DARK SECRETS OF THE TURF

DARK SECRETS OF THE TURF

John White

(Former Magazine Sports Writer of the Year
and author of *The Racegoers' Encyclopedia*)

Rushmere Wynne Limited

First published 1991 (Rosters Ltd.)
This edition 1996

ISBN 0 948035 32 3

Published in the UK by
RUSHMERE WYNNE Limited
4-5 Harmill, Grovebury Road
Leighton Buzzard
Bedfordshire, LU7 8FF
Telephone: 01525 853726
Facsimile: 01525 852037

Design by MacWing

Printed and bound in Great Britain by
HS Printers Limited
4-5 Harmill, Grovebury Road
Leighton Buzzard
Bedfordshire, LU7 8FF

About the Author

John White is a former Magazine Sports Writer of the Year. A past contributor to the *Sporting Life Weekender*, the *Sporting Life*, the *Observer Colour Supplement*, the *Sunday Telegraph*, *Competition Rider, Royalty Monthly, The Lady, Equestrian World, Mensa*, the *Betting Man's Contact*, the *Irish Post*, *Sportscene*, and to *Racing Monthly*, and *Turf and Track* as its systems expert, he is happy to combine journalism with examining and lecturing in English Literature and lives at Falmouth. He is also the author of *Racing Systems with the Pocket Calculator* and of the HarperCollins *Racegoers' Encyclopedia.*

For my wife and family, in memory of my mother and
with special thanks to Derrick.

Introduction

Written by the former systems expert of *Racing Monthly,* this revolutionary book, now extensively revised and updated since first appearing in 1991, reveals the 'dark secrets' that so often lie behind success on the turf. As a compendium of advanced winner-finding strategies, it is unrivalled for the sheer depth of its research, its entertaining style and thought-provoking insights. Especially written to appeal to the already very knowledgeable as well as the novice racing fan, it may well become the bane of bookmakers since it provides those battling against them with extremely powerful ammunition.

CONTENTS

PART ONE: TRAINERS' TACTICS

PART TWO: SIDING WITH JOCKEYS

PART THREE: EXPLOITING RACEDAY FACTORS

PART ONE: TRAINERS' TACTICS

STRATEGY 1:

Profiting from Habits and Preferences

In one of the most entertaining of horse racing stories, *Little Miss Universe,* William Saroyan describes a horse player called the 'Barrel' whose desire, given his belief that the horses were 'mere puppets, helpless and a bit foolish', was to discover 'the *dark secrets* and tendencies of the owner and trainer of the horse.' Interestingly, many systematic approaches to winner finding do *not* involve racehorses, but their 'connections' – the many men and women who can be assumed to have a vested interest in their success. That on the turf there is a good deal to gain from the study of human, as opposed to equine, behaviour is demonstrated by the commercial success of several guides which consider the strategies and performances of trainers. The best known of these are annual publications such as the *Sporting Life's Trainers' Review.* Moreover, in John Whitley's massive annual compilation, *Computer Racing Form,* a significant amount of space is devoted to data that does much to pinpoint trainers' partialities.

The rationale behind all these rigorous analyses of the particular ploys of racehorse handlers is, of course, that they are methodical businessmen and women who act out of habit and that if their habits have been repeatedly successful, horses involved in them in future will be worth backing. One of the most potentially profitable strategies involving trainers' past behaviour is based on the belief that the arrival of certain horseboxes on certain racecourses can provide particularly profitable pointers. Indeed, research has shown that there is often a close correlation between some trainers' successes and the preferences they have expressed for certain tracks, which may well be the reason why several leading handlers seem actually reluctant to nominate their favourite venues! However, sufficient trainers have revealed where they most relish success and ample data is available on their past triumphs for a select list of 'trainers for courses' to be compiled.

I find that there is nothing quite so enthralling as using this list. Firstly, I check to see whether the trainers I know will at least *enjoy* revisiting certain venues (since they have been the scenes of many of their past successes) are due to have runners on these courses and, secondly, I assess whether any of these runners merit support. Perhaps the most illuminating way of explaining how you can benefit from this strategy is to mention the conclusions I reached about some races run recently at Warwick:

WARWICK

COURSE SPECIALISTS

TRAINERS	Wins	Rnrs	%	JOCKEYS	Winners	Rides	%
M Pipe	30	117	25.6	A P McCoy	3	13	23.1
Miss H Knight	8	33	24.2	T Jenks	8	36	22.2
D Nicholson	24	106	22.6	R Johnson	4	21	19.0
O Sherwood	10	48	20.8	J Osborne	15	83	18.1
N Henderson	9	46	19.6	A Maguire	14	79	17.7
Mrs J Pitman	16	86	18.6	M Dwyer	3	17	17.6

1.50 CRECY JUVENILE NOVICES HURDLE (4-Y-0: £2,448: 2m) (12 runners)

1	21P0	CHICODARI 16 (B,D,S) (Brig C Harvey) D Nicholson 11-5	A Maguire	99
2	1	HAMILTON SILK 40 (G) (Elite Racing Club) M Pipe 11-5	J Osborne	80
3	5410P	LAST SPIN 3 (B,D,G) (Mrs E Long) J Jenkins 11-0	R Supple	77
4	UF0	BOURDONNER 16 (Million In Mind Partnership) W Jenks 10-12	W Marston	62
5		ENCHANTED COTTAGE 114F (David Kay Racing) M Hammond 10-12	A P McCoy	–
6	02	INDICATOR 16 (Lady Anne Bentinck) J Quinn 10-12	M Dwyer	90
7		MENOO WHO 147F (Jebel Ali Racing Stables) D Nicholson 10-12	R Johnson (3)	–
8	40	MIM-LOU-AND 21 (J Martin) Miss H Knight 10-12	J F Titley	90
9	3U	RALITSA 9 (Wetherby Racing Bureau 25) M Hammond 10-12	R Garritty	90
10	0	SELATAN 9 (Starlight Racing) D Gandolfo 10-12	D Leahy	66
11	062	SHEPHERDS REST 9 (The Odd Dozen) S Mellor 10-12	N Mann	86
12	0	CHARM DANCER 115F (Mrs R Cobbold) M Pipe 10-7	J Lower	–

BETTING: 11-4 Chicodari, 7-2 Indicator, 4-1 Menoo Who, 5-1 Hamilton Silk, 7-1 Shepherds Rest, 8-1 Ralitsa, 10-1 Last Spin, 12-1 others.

1995: NO CORRESPONDING MEETING

FORM FOCUS

CHICODARI short-head 2nd of 12 to Talk Balk (placings later reversed) in juvenile hurdle at Cheltenham (2m 110yd, good to soft). HAMILTON SILK beat Granique 1¼l in 18-runner Bangor selling novice hurdle (2m 1f, good). LAST SPIN beat Battleship Bruce neck in 9-runner Fakenham juvenile hurdle (2m, good). INDICATOR 1¼l 2nd of 14 to Volunteer in Warwick juvenile hurdle (2m, good to soft) with SHEPHERD'S REST 28l 6th. MENOO WHO 2l 2nd of 8 to Khayrawani in Flat maiden at Roscommon (1m 4f, firm). MIM-LOU-AND 11l 4th of 20 to Sovereigns Parade in juvenile hurdle at Haydock (2m, good) penultimate start with INDICATOR 32l 10th. RALITSA 1l and neck 3rd of 24 to Elation in juvenile hurdle at Newcastle (2m, good) penultimate start. SHEPHERDS REST 6l 2nd of 17 to Mistinguett in juvenile hurdle at Warwick (2m, good to soft) with SELATAN 20l 8th and RALITSA unseated rider 3rd.
Selection: INDICATOR

2.20 BLENHEIM NOVICES CHASE (£3,066: 3m 2f) (4 runners)

1	4/FU23-1	CELTIC TOWN 45 (F,S) (Lady Helen Smith) O Sherwood 8-11-11	J A McCarthy	82
2	00-321F	FIXTURESSECRETARY 18 (G,S) (K Manley) D Nicholson 7-11-11	A Maguire	75
3	215-1P1	IDIOT'S LADY 17 (G,S) (Mrs J Ollivant) Mrs J Pitman 7-11-6	W Marston	99
4	0/2P/	ADMIRAL VILLENEUVE 803 (Mrs W Macauley) C Egerton 8-11-5	J Osborne	–

BETTING: 4-6 Idiot's Lady, 3-1 Fixturessecretary, 7-2 Celtic Town, 20-1 Admiral Villeneuve.

FORM FOCUS

CELTIC TOWN beat Le Meille 2½l in 4-runner novice chase at Doncaster (3m, good to firm). FIXTURESSECRETARY best effort this season, 3l 2nd of 7 to Challenger Du Luc in Leicester novice chase (2m 4f, good to firm). IDIOT'S LADY beat Sister Stephanie 4l in 13-runner novice chase at Towcester (2m 6f, soft). ADMIRAL VILLENEUVE 15l 2nd of 11 to Shaffic in Wetherby novice hurdle (2m 4f, good) penultimate start, Oct 1993.
Selection: IDIOT'S LADY (nap)

2.50 TRAFALGAR NOVICES CHASE (£3,037: 2m) (8 runners)

1	/0623/P	ARMATEUR 11 (Major H Porter) J McConnochie 8-11-4	R Bellamy	–
2	11004-3	BIG STRAND 67 (BF,S) (E Jones) M Pipe 7-11-4	J Lower	–
3	P0-6	COOLINNY 39 (D McCain) D McCain 7-11-4	D McCain	–
4	0/00P0-6	COUNTRY KEEPER 13 (B Ryall) B Ryall 8-11-4	G Upton	64
5	0-P00	DARK DIAMOND 9 (Mrs S Kavanagh) H Kavanagh 6-11-4	A S Smith	–
6	0-33334	MHEMEANLES 18 (F) (G Farndon) Capt J Wilson 6-11-4	R Johnson (3)	71
7	652355	MUST BE MAGICAL 6 (F,S) (P Bradley) P Bradley 8-11-4	B Harding (3)	83
8	04-124F	THE CAUMRUE 9 (G,S) (The On The Run Partnership) G Balding 8-11-4	A P McCoy	99

BETTING: 4-5 Big Strand, 2-1 The Caumrue, 7-1 Must Be Magical, 8-1 Mhemeanles, 16-1 others.

FORM FOCUS

ARMATEUR 20l 3rd of 18 to Greenhil Tare Away in novice hurdle at Worcester (3m, good) penultimate start, April 1994. BIG STRAND 12l 3rd of 7 to Eskimo Nel in a handicap hurdle here (2m, good). MHEMEANLES 9½l 4th of 7 to Lochnagrain in a novice chase at Sedgefield (2m 1f, good to firm). MUST BE MAGICAL 6¼l 5th of 11 to Stormy Coral in a handicap chase at Carlisle (2m, good to soft). THE CAUMRUE 7¾l 4th of 13 to Major Summit in a novice chase at Sandown (2m 4f 110yd, good to soft) penultimate start.
Selection: THE CAUMRUE

3.20 AGINCOURT HANDICAP CHASE (£3,711: 3m 2f) (7 runners)

1	4131/R0	THE WIDGET MAN 16 (D,F,G,S) (A Ilsley) J Gifford 10-12-0	L Aspell (5)	96
2	322-P54	DIAMOND FORT 7 (D,F,G,S) (Mrs R Stocks) J McConnochie 11-10-13	A Maguire	96
3	0223-11	NICKLUP 33 (F,G,S) (Lord Cadogan) T Forster 9-10-12	A Thornton	94
4	220F1F-	SPARROW HALL 266 (F,G,S) (P Hall) J Fitzgerald 9-10-5	M Dwyer	99
5	315-1P6	DISTINCTIVE 9 (S) (J Hancock) M Wilkinson 7-10-1	J F Titley	98
6	1U-532U	ALICE SMITH 9 (G,S) (Mrs J Eckley) B Eckley 9-10-0	W McFarland	86
7	322-500	MISS FERN 37 (F,G,S) (Mrs P Andrews) R Dickin 11-10-0	D Meredith	79

Long handicap: Alice Smith 9-6, Miss Fern 8-11.

BETTING: 7-4 Nicklup, 7-2 Sparrow Hall, 5-1 The Widget Man, 6-1 Diamond Fort, Distinctive, 10-1 Alice Smith, 25-1 Miss Fern.

FORM FOCUS

THE WIDGET MAN 59l 17th of 26 to Buckhouse Boy in handicap hurdle here (2m 4f 110yd, good to soft). Best effort over fences, beat Indian Tonic 10l in a 4-runner handicap chase at Sandown (3m 110yd, good to soft). DIAMOND FORT 29l 4th of 11 to Nazzaro in a handicap chase at Fontwell (3m 2f 110yd, soft). NICKLUP, completed double, beat ALICE SMITH (7lb worse off) neck in a 7-runner handicap chase at Ludlow (3m, good). SPARROW HALL beat Dominant Serenade short-head in a 10-runner novice chase at Carlisle (3m, good to firm) on penultimate start, April 1995. DISTINCTIVE best effort this season, beat Change The Act ½l in a 9-runner handicap chase at Bangor (2m 4f 110yd, good to soft).

Selection: NICKLUP

3.50 ALAMEIN NOVICES HURDLE (£2,594: 2m 4f 110yd) (22 runners)

1	5561-0	CLAVERHOUSE 11 (F) (Mrs P Corbett) J Fitzgerald 7-11-7	M Dwyer	--
2	U-3340	DJAIS 9 (T Long) J Jenkins 7-11-7	G Bradley	90
3	63	FLYING GUNNER 11 (R Green) D Nicholson 5-11-7	A Maguire	84
4	00	GREY STORY 16 (G Phillips) A J Wilson 8-11-7	T Jenks	65
5	0-0	MUSIC THERAPY 56 (R Van Gelder) T Forster 6-11-7	A Thornton	--
6	U	NAUTICAL GEORGE 18 (Mrs E Ellis) J Upson 6-11-7	R Supple	--
7		ONE MORE MAN (A Ilsley) J Gifford 5-11-7	L Aspell (5)	--
8	30-F464	REVEREND BROWN 16 (J Palmer-Brown) O Sherwood 6-11-7	J Osborne	89
9	0	SEA FREEDOM 9 (Miss B Swire) G Balding 5-11-7	A P McCoy	--
10	0/PP-P	THE ELOPER 39 (Miss E England) Miss E England 8-11-7	P Crowley (7)	--
11	0-0	THE NAUGHTY VICAR 37 (The Hell Raisers) S Mellor 6-11-7	N Mann	--
12	4/40	TREMBLE 11 (Mrs E Roberts) N Henderson 7-11-7	M A Fitzgerald	--
13	0020	WEEHEBY 9 (The DANA Partnership) M Barraclough 7-11-7	R Garritty	86
14	2	BROGEEN LADY 62 (Starlight Racing) D Gandolfo 6-11-2	D Leahy	99
15	240200	COMEDY HOUR 32 (N Rolfe) P Murphy 5-11-2	W Marston	53
16	00	EMMA GRIMES 11 (M Holder) J Moore 5-11-2	W McFarland	58
17	0/P	FORTITUDE STAR 59 (Mrs J Saunders) Mrs R Henderson 6-11-2	B Fenton (5)	--
18	2F303	MOONLIGHT AIR 37 (Mrs P Badger) J Spearing 5-11-2	R Johnson (3)	84
19	0-00PP	PARTY BEDLAM 13 (Mrs S Walters) C James 7-11-2	Mr E James	--
20	/3/3S-5P	SPRING GRASS 16 (B Ryall) B Ryall 8-11-2	G Upton	67
21	P	CHELWORTH WOLF 32 (R Giles) J Spearing 4-10-8	J Lodder	--
22	00	LORD FREDERICK 46 (D Dutton) Miss S Wilton 4-10-8	Gary Lyons	64

BETTING: 3-1 Brogeen Lady, 4-1 Reverend Brown, 9-2 Flying Gunner, 6-1 Tremble, 7-1 One More Man, 8-1 Weeheby, 12-1 Comedy Hour, 14-1 others.

FORM FOCUS

CLAVERHOUSE 43l 7th of 13 to Lansborough in a novice hurdle at Wetherby (2m 4f 110yd, good to soft). DJAIS 25l 7th of 20 to Wisley Wonder in a novice hurdle at Ascot (2m 4f, soft) with SEA FREEDOM 31l 16th. FLYING GUNNER 10½l 3rd of 14 to Simply Dashing in a novice hurdle at Wetherby (2m 4f 110yd, good to soft). REVEREND BROWN 9l 4th of 22 to Goldenswift in a novices' handicap hurdle at Sandown (2m 6f, good to soft), SPRING GRASS (9lb better off) tailed off when pulled up after 5th. TREMBLE 33l 9th of 17 to Wild West Wind in a novice hurdle at Wincanton (2m, good to soft). WEEHEBY 1¾l 2nd of 16 to Serious in a novice hurdle at Uttoxeter (2m, good to firm) on penultimate start with MOONLIGHT AIR 12l 3rd. BROGEEN LADY 4l 2nd of 5 to Wisley Wonder in a novice hurdle at Cheltenham (3m 2f, good).

Selection: BROGEEN LADY

4.20 WATERLOO HANDICAP HURDLE (£2,710: 2m) (8 runners)

1	000-203	MISTER DRUM 58 (D,G,S) (M Batchelor) M Wilkinson /-12-0	P Crowley (7)	99
2	212161	MOST EQUAL 16 (CD,F,S) (H Kirpalani) M Pipe 6-11-11	J Lower	95
3	2/3FF51	ERLKING 11F (B,D,G) (S Tindall) S Mellor 6-11-1	N Mann	96
4	02/31-00	SECRETARY OF STATE 18F (D,G) (W Ponsonby) D Arbuthnot 10-10-12	J Osborne	83
5	242-402	GOLDINGO 4 (D,S) (G Price) G Price 9-10-11	A P McCoy	96
6	30421-0	BARQAISH 9 (G) (K Dale) M Barraclough 9-10-2	G Lee (3)	88
7	U21P-FF	RAINHAM 34 (D,S) (A Collins) D McCain 9-10-0	A Maguire	--
8	/403P0	PUSEY STREET BOY 4 (D,F) (C Marks (Banbury)) J Bosley 9-10-0	I Lawrence	--

Long handicap: Rainham 9-3, Pusey Street Boy 8-11.

BETTING: 6-4 Most Equal, 5-2 Mister Drum, 4-1 Erlking, 7-1 Goldingo, 8-1 Secretary Of State, 12-1 Barqaish, 14-1 Pusey Street Boy, 20-1 Rainham.

Fortunately, in being aware that, according to up-to-date statistics appearing in my daily copy of *The Times*, trainers Martin Pipe, Jenny Pitman and David Nicholson were not only rated as in the top six handlers for Warwick, but were sending out runners that were either given a top rating of 99 by this newspaper's private handicapper or forecast to start favourite. I made an especial note of Chicodari in the 1.50, Idiot's Lady in the 2.20, Big Strand in the 2.50 and Most Equal in the 4.20. This strategy was well and truly vindicated as Chicodari won at 7–2, Idiot's Lady at 8–13 and Big Strand at a better than forecast price of 7–4. Indeed, had Most Equal managed to win the last race at Warwick, the top trainers for courses strategy would have been astoundingly successful!

WARWICK

Going: GOOD

1.50 (2m nov hdle): **CHICODARI** (A Maguire, 7-2F) 1; **Hamilton Silk** (5-1) 2; **Ralitsa** (9-2) 3. 12 ran. 5, 3½. (D Nicholson). Tote: win £4.00; places £2.00, £2.20, £2.20. Dual F'cast: £9.90. CSF: £21.89. Trio: £17.50.

2.20 (3m2f nov ch): **IDIOT'S LADY** (W Marston, 8-13F) 1; **Fixturessecretary** (4-1) 2; **Celtic Town** (7-2) 3. 4 ran. 2½, 20. (Mrs J Pitman). Tote: win £1.70. Dual F'cast: £2.30. CSF: £3.26.

2.50 (2m nov ch): **BIG STRAND** (J Lower, 7-4) 1; **Coolinny** (50-1) 2; **Must Be Magical** (10-1) 3. 8 ran. The Caumrue 4-5F. 3½, 1¼. (M Pipe). Tote: win £2.20; places £1.50, £4.70, £2.60. Dual F'cast. £68.30. CSF: £52.44.

3.20 (3m2f h'cap ch): **DIAMOND FORT** (A Maguire, 11-1) 1; **Distinctive** (4-1) 2; **Alice Smith** (15-2) 3. 7 ran. Sparrow Hall 9-4F. 3½, dist. (J McConnochie). Tote: win £14.30; places £3.20, £2.80. Dual F'cast: £16.20. CSF: £51.72.

3.50 (2m4f110y nov hdle): **DJAIS** (G Bradley, 7-2) 1; **Flying Gunner** (11-2) 2; **Moonlight Air** (16-1) 3. 22 ran. Brogeen Lady 100-30F. 5, 1¼. (J Jenkins). Tote: win £4.60; places £2.00, £2.00, £4.30. Dual F'cast: £16.40. CSF: £24.43. Trio: £220.00.

4.20 (2m h'cap hdle): **RAINHAM** (A Maguire, 33-1) 1; **Goldingo** (9-2) 2; **Pusey Street Boy** (33-1) 3. 8 ran. Most Equal 9-4F. 3, 1½. (D McCain). Tote: win £20.10; places £3.30, £1.80, £3.30. Dual F'cast: £33.50. CSF: £167.76. Tricast: £4,512.36.

QUADPOT: £119.70. PLACEPOT: £313.60.

Rather than present a list of trainers for courses that over time (as happened to that appearing in the first edition of this book) would inevitably tend to date, I recommend daily reference to the updated trainer statistics in *The Times* and the adoption of the selection strategy explained and exemplified above which ensures that runners sent out by handlers with the best updated past course records are supported if they are top-rated by form experts or betting forecast compilers.

STRATEGY 2:

The Anniversary Approach and the Farming of Races

Some knowledgeable backers subscribe to the 'anniversary method' of racehorse selection and one refined application of this involves looking for fancied runners in races that a particular trainer has made a habit of winning year after year. Such so-called 'farming' of certain contests is by no means as rare as you might expect. Indeed, you have only to look at the results of Doncaster's May Hill Stakes to discover the amazing achievement of Henry Cecil in training seven of its ten winners between 1982 and 1991. Cecil's record in another Doncaster race, the Racing Post Trophy, staged in October is also so impressive as to guarantee that I always scrutinise the claims of any runner he sends to race in this top-class event.

Fortunately, it is relatively simple to detect which handlers, like Martin Pipe in the Welsh Grand National, are fond of 'farming' the most prestigious races, since their many past runnings are documented in annual publications and two specialist racing journalists, Gerald Delamere in the *Sporting Life* and Craig Thake in the *Racing Post*, specialise in trying to find pointers to their impending winners in past copies of the form books. Thake's *10 Year Trends* feature appears in a most useful tabular form and thus trainers who farm for the richest harvest can be rapidly identified.

STRATEGY 3:

Races for Trainers

Everything in this life is, of course, relative – as well as 6–4 against, as Damon Runyon once put it so tellingly. I have found that farming much humbler races than the May Hill Stakes can feature in the strategies of trainers with smaller strings than Henry Cecil. Indeed, delving into past copies of form books I have discovered that some racecourse trainers, often female ones, seem particularly determined to win certain races. Not long ago, for example, my homework convinced me that Open University graduate Mrs. C. Reavey would do her utmost to win the race staged at Salisbury in memory of her late husband. The horse in question was in fact 'pushed out' to prevail by a neck, after its opening odds had been most significantly forced down by over 50% from a most welcome opening rate of 16–1!

The strong family reasons that induce certain trainers to make particularly determined efforts to win certain races often involve fathers who, understandably, like nothing better than to see winners ridden home by their darling daughters. Indeed, top trainer Guy Harwood paid a very rare visit to Warwick's lowly racecourse early one summer (a week after his elder daughter Amanda had been beaten by a neck there) to watch his younger daughter Gaye compete in a National Hunt flat race that formed a most Corinthian finale to a rather lacklustre evening card. As it happened, his presence did much to cause Midlands bookmakers to offer rather cramped odds against her mount, As You Were, which was definitely all the rage in the ring. Sadly, perhaps, it was her memory of how her father's jockey, Greville Starkey, had lost the Derby by adopting waiting tactics on Dancing Brave in the same distinctive red and green colours of Khaled Abdulla that she was sporting, that led the determined Gaye to try to make all and then, ironically, to be beaten by the same minuscule margin that had prevented her father's stable from landing one of the heaviest Derby gambles of the post-war period! Thus, 'As You Were' proved the order of the day for the Harwood family and Guy himself was glimpsed philosophically resorting to a little liquid (possibly Southern) Comfort as I left the scene of his second Waterloo at Warwick within a week! My feeling was that as he left he was already planning a retrieval mission and this was confirmed by his post-race comment to a *Sporting Life* reporter that 'we will win this race next year'. Thus almost straight from the horse's mouth, even if in narrow defeat, came words indicating the wisdom of analysing the predilections of racehorse trainers!

Rather than aim at particular contests for which they may sometimes 'lay out' horses all season, some trainers seem to make almost super-human efforts to be successful at *one meeting* of the many held on a racecourse each season. In this connection, not long ago I noticed that Mrs. Rosemary Lomax, who used to train in a modest way at Baydon near Marlborough, had succeeded in producing a winner at Lingfield's early August meeting year after year. Having accomplished this feat in three successive years, Mrs. Lomax looked to have a truly outstanding chance of pulling off a four-timer since, in a match that opened the card in question, she could be seen to be the trainer of the favourite and clear form choice, Silmira. Indeed, my research on Mrs. Lomax's record at this particular fixture confirmed my feeling that Silmira was as near a 'racing certainty' as I was likely to see for many a season. In the event, he did prove rather more successful than the 20–1 on chance that once deposited Sir Gordon Richards at the start of another two horse race at Chepstow. Indeed, by winning at the far more generous odds of 10–11, co-favourite Silmira did put some cash in my bank balance, although as he scrambled home by only a head I was left wondering about the soundness of my strategy until the last second of the race.

STRATEGY 4:

Trainers' Multiple Winners

Winners last time out are obviously well worth serious consideration. Indeed, this belief was one of the original foundations of 'Fineform'. The problem here, of course, is determining whether a previously successful runner has a really good chance of following up, but, fortunately, there is a way out of this. This involves knowing which trainers have the ability to send out prolific winners.

Most usefully, such information was recently made available via a most useful *Racing Post* feature: 'Trainers with Prolific Winners'. Some of the handlers mentioned in this, most notably Bill O'Gorman (whose Provideo has had a race named after him for winning 16 times in 1984 and whose Timeless Times emulated this feat in 1990), Jack Berry, Barry Hills, Richard Hannon, Martin Pipe, Mark Johnston, Henry Cecil and Sir Mark Prescott (whose Spindrifter won thirteen races in 1980), have been identified as adept in getting their horses to win at least two races in a row.

Thus on any racing day, if I notice that any of these trainers is fielding a runner – especially a two-year-old unsoured by many seasons of racing or an older, more experienced sprinter – that is bidding to augment its first success of the season or a win last time out that is not the sequel to a previous success, then I give it my support.

For example, at a recent late season Newmarket meeting I noticed that in the second race Mark Johnston was fielding a runner that was aiming to supplement a single success that it had registered on its debut. Polar Eclipse was, in fact, a clear Strategy 4 qualifier on this account and so I had no hesitation in making him the subject of a sizeable wager before he won readily at 100–30.

Incidentally, my confidence in Polar Eclipse was greatly increased when I noticed that he was also a Strategy 3 qualifier, as his trainer had succeeded in winning the Asko Appliances Zetland Stakes the previous season with Double Eclipse!

2.10 *Asko Appliances Zetland Stakes (Class A) (Listed Race)* **CH4**
6 declared *Winner £9,246* **1m2f Row**

£15,000 added **For** 2yo **Weights** colts and geldings 8st 11lb; fillies 8st 6lb **Penalties** a winner of a Class C race 3lb; of a Listed race or Class B race 5lb; of a Pattern race 7lb **Entries** 8 pay £150 **Penalty Value 1st** £9,246 **2nd** £3,414 **3rd** £1,632 **4th** £660 **5th** £255 **6th** £93

1 (6)	533111 **WEET-A-MINUTE (IRE)** 12 *ro c Nabeel Dancer–Ludovica* **R Hollinshead** Ed Weetman (Haulage & Storage) Ltd	2 9-2 **T Ives**	105
2 (1)	5 **ATHENRY** 32 *b c Siberian Express–Heresheis* **J Pearce** A J Thompson	2 8-11 **G Bardwell**	98
3 (5)	133 **EXALTED (IRE)** 8 *b c High Estate–Heavenward* **Sir M Prescott** Mrs F R Watts	2 8-11 **G Duffield**	105
4 (4)	7231 **GENTILHOMME** 33 D *ch c Generous–Bold Flawless* **P F I Cole** H R H Prince Fahd Salman	2 8-11 **T Quinn**	104
5 (2)	1 **POLAR ECLIPSE** 17 *ch c Polar Falcon–Princess Zepoli* **M Johnston** J R Good	2 8-11 **J Reid**	107
6 (3)	555 **ZAFORUM** 19 *b c Deploy–Beau's Delight* **L Montague Hall** The Forum Ltd	2 8-11 **B Doyle**	93

1994 (9 ran) **Double Eclipse** (5) M Johnston 2 8-9 PM102 ✕ J Weaver 4/1C

BETTING FORECAST: 9-4 Polar Eclipse, 5-2 Weet-A-Minute, 11-4 Gentilhomme, 9-2 Exalted, 14 Athenry, 33 Zaforum.

STRATEGY 5:

Monitoring Trainers' Entries

There is yet another aspect of a trainer's recent behaviour, as opposed to that adopted in a previous season, that some analysts consider offers a key to his or her future success. These individuals make up the staff of Future Form – a service based on the belief that much can be learned about a trainer's estimations of truly 'dark horses' – his or her untried or inexperienced charges – by studying the value and importance of the races in which they have been (often expensively) entered to run in future. This monitoring of the 'great expectations' of racehorse handlers amounts to such a sophisticated bid to divine yet more of the dark secrets of racehorse handlers that its originator has written a full-blown treatise on the often fascinating business of what he designates as 'racehorse evaluation by entry analysis'. Subscribers to the Future Form service (of 82 Girton Road, Cambridge) are offered the opportunity to discover trainers' opinions of their best charges and to identify a stable's potential stars before they run, via a weekly updated analysis of trainers' entries.

The rationale behind this computer-based, most ingenious and potentially very profitable way of 'tracking' trainers' entries is sound. Information provided by Future Form can be put to even more profitable use if you know which trainers are adept at sending out first-time-out winners and, in this connection, the following list of trainers, who either specialise in pulling off this difficult feat or also profit doubly from it by betting, may well prove invaluable.

FLAT

D. Arbuthnot*
R. Armstrong*
A. Bailey*
R. Bastiman*
M. Bell*
C. Booth*
R. Boss*
N. Bycroft*
H. Candy*
H. Cecil
D. Chapman*
T. Craig*
C. Cyzer*
J. Fitzgerald
J. Gosden*
Miss S. Hall*
B. Hanbury*
G. Harwood*
L. Holt*
Lord Huntingdon*
W. Jarvis*
P. Kelleway*
P. Makin*
B. McMahon*
D. Morley*
C. Nelson*
M. O'Neill*
J. Parkes*
M. Pipe*
M. Prescott*

NATIONAL HUNT

R. Akehurst*
D. Barons
J. Edwards*
D. Elsworth*
C. Egerton
J. Gifford
J. Johnson
D. Murray–Smith
M. Pipe*
Mrs. J. Pitman
J. White*

Mrs. J. Ramsden*
Miss L. Sidall*
H. Thompson-Jones*
C. Thornton*
M. Tomkins*
J. Watts*
J. White*
G. Wragg*

** Market support often significant.*

The staff of Future Form are not alone in seeing the wisdom of monitoring the future engagements of racehorses. One 'do-it-yourself' method of doing just that which I have devised capitalises on the belief that horses will be quite expensively entered for races at a future point when their trainers adjudge they will be fully 'wound up' and fit to run for their lives. Since purchase of Future Form's bible the *Racing Calendar* is expensive and the *Raceform Handicap Book* no longer prints a whole week's forthcoming entries, purchase of the latter (or the *Weekender* on Thursday, or the *Sporting Life* on Friday and the *Racing Post* on Monday) can reveal horses with multiple engagements in the very near future. What you need to note is which particular race or two (or even more – each obliging connections to pay to stand their ground prior to the final overnight declaration stage) a trainer has finally decided to pick. Once final running plans can be seen (first in an evening paper published almost 24 hours before racing) and then confirmed in the next day's daily newspaper, you can start comparing the race finally chosen by the trainer with the alternative contest(s) he or she has discarded and try to divine the train of thought that led to this decision.

From this particular attempt to learn yet more of the dark secrets of racing stables two types of final running plans – either to allow a horse to compete in one race rather than another at the same meeting, or in one staged at one particular meeting, rather than elsewhere – will emerge. I suggest that in order to narrow down the number of horses in which to take an interest you concentrate on those which are returned as favourites, which suggests that they may be enjoying stable support.

Another vivid and most profitable vindication of the wisdom of supporting any runner that has held more than one engagement at the *same meeting,* if it receives market support in its chosen race, was provided at Stratford. As can be seen from the following two pages of the *Weekender* published two days before this was due to be staged, only four horses, Daily Sport Soon, Karnatak, Light Dancer and Legal Tina, were doubly engaged and the last two mentioned (the only ones whose odds shortened in the course betting) duly won as the 11–4 favourite and the 11–1 springer respectively. This was reported a few days later by the author of the *Racing and Football Outlook's* 'Ring Wrinkles' feature.

> *Up at Stratford over the sticks there was all kind of action in the ring. Legal Tina came down from 7–1 to 11–4 before her fluent victory in the 2m claiming hurdle. Light Dancer, trained by Liam Codd, gave the ring a pasting when taking the 2m handicap hurdle.*
>
> *The gelding had previously been pulled up on the all–weather at Southwell, but there was plenty of confidence behind him and he was backed from 25–1 to 10's, eventually returning 11–1.*

SATURDAY'S RUNNERS INDEX

A

Able Jet (USA)...4.30 Thi 1
Absent Forever..4.30 Thi 2
Acqua Noir......2.30 Sou 1
Adeline Lynn.....3.45 Str 1
Adwick Park......4.00 Thi 1
African Chimes 5.15 Kem 1
African Chimes 2.30 Sou 2
Age Of Miracles 4.45 Kem 1
Air Nymph.......2.15 Kem 1
Al Badeto.........4.00 Sou 1
Albadr (USA)...4.15 Kem 1
Alberta Henrietta 2.30 Sou 3
Aldwick Colonnade ....2.45 Kem 1
Alexandra Katrine ....4.00 Sou 2
Alicante ....4.45 Str 1
Alles-Oops.........2.15 Hay 1
All Fired Up ....3.30 Thi 1
Allinson's Mate (IRE) ....3.15 Kem 1
All Welcome.....5.15 Kem 3
Almasa ....3.15 Kem 2
Al Skeet (USA) 5.15 Kem 2
Amasake ....2.30 Sou 4
American Connexion ....3.45 Kem 1
Anatroccolo .....2.45 Kem 2
Angel Bright.....5.00 Sou 1
Angelica Park....3.00 Thi 1
Ankara's Princess (USA) ....4.50 Hay 1
Anna Karietta..2.15 Kem 2
Annie McGrath ..3.45 Str 2
Anstey Boy.......2.45 Str 1
Arabat ....2.30 Thi 1
Arbor Vitae......2.00 Thi 1
Arbor Vitae......2.00 Thi 2
Arturian ....4.30 Thi 3
Ash Amour......2.45 Kem 3
Ash Amour......5.15 Kem 4
Ash Amour......2.30 Sou 5
Asterix ....3.15 Kem 3
Astrid Gilberto...4.45 Str 2
Athens Gate (USA) ....3.45 Str 3
Athlon.............2.30 Thi 2
At Peace..........4.50 Hay 2
Ave Valeque (USA) ....4.20 Hay 1
Avoca Holmes...5.00 Sou 2
Ayr Classic.......4.20 Hay 2
Ayr Raider.......4.50 Hay 3
Ayr Raider.......2.30 Thi 3
Azmaam (USA)...3.50 Hay 1

B

Babarooms Paradise (NZ) ....4.45 Str 3
Bad Trade.........4.15 Str 1
Balanced Realm (USA) ....4.00 Sou 3
Balanced Realm (USA) ....2.45 Str 4
Balasani (FR)...4.45 Kem 2
Baldski Boy (USA) ....3.30 Sou 1
Bankroll..........3.45 Kem 2
Banksy Boy (IRE) 3.00 Sou 1
Barcham...........4.45 Str 4
Barford Lad.....3.45 Kem 3
Barkston Singer 2.45 Kem 4
Barlogan ....3.30 Sou 2
Baroness Gymcrak ....4.00 Sou 4
Barrish...........4.45 Kem 3
Barron's Boy....3.30 Sou 3
Barsac.............3.00 Sou 2
Bashaq ....5.15 Kem 5
Basic Thoughts..4.30 Sou 1
Battle Of Flowers ....2.45 Kem 5
Battle Of Flowers 2.30 Thi 4
Battle On.........2.00 Thi 2
Baylis ....3.50 Hay 2
Bayford Prince (IRE) ....5.00 Thi 1
Bay Runner....2.15 Kem 3
Bdoore (IRE) ....5.00 Thi 2
Bean Boy.........3.00 Thi 3
Beau Benz.......5.00 Sou 3
Beau Venture (USA) ....4.30 Thi 4
Beebob ....5.00 Thi 3
Beech Park.......4.15 Str 2
Belle Danseuse..4.20 Hay 3
Bellefan (IRE)...3.30 Sou 5
Belle Of Steel ...3.00 Sou 3
Bell Turret.......4.45 Str 5
Beltalong.........5.00 Sou 4
Be Magic.........3.30 Sou 4
Ben's Birdie .....3.00 Thi 4
Best Effort ......4.45 Kem 4
Bestow ....1.45 Hay 1
Bickerman........5.15 Str 1
Bidweaya (USA) 2.45 Kem 6
Bidweaya (USA) 2.30 Sou 6
Bifocal ....5.00 Sou 5
Big Blow.........3.20 Hay 1
Big Blow.........3.15 Kem 4
Big Idea...........3.30 Sou 7
Bilsha ....5.15 Str 2
Birling Ashes...3.15 Kem 5
Birthday Parade (USA) ....2.45 Kem 7
Bit Of A Lark.....4.30 Thi 5
Blake's Treasure 5.15 Kem 6
Blazing Horseshoe ....3.30 Sou 6
Blue Aeroplane 4.20 Hay 4
Bluefontaine....5.15 Kem 7
Blushing Red....4.30 Sou 2
Bold Ambition...3.50 Hay 3
Bold Double ....4.20 Hay 5
Bold Relative....2.30 Thi 5
Bold Spark.......3.00 Sou 4
Bonnie Boy ......3.45 Str 5
Bonnie Kate......3.00 Sou 5
Bonny Rose......5.00 Sou 6
Boules.............3.45 Kem 4
Brantfell ....4.30 Thi 6
Brave Question (USA) ....4.30 Sou 3
Break Loose.....4.00 Sou 5
Bright Sapphire..3.45 Str 6
Broad Beam......3.15 Str 1
Broom Isle.......4.00 Thi 2
Broughtino ......5.15 Kem 8
Brown Fairy (USA) ....4.00 Thi 3
Bubulina ....2.45 Kem 8
Bursana...........5.00 Sou 7
Bu-Sofyan ....5.15 Kem 9
Busted Rock ...4.45 Kem 5
Buster ....4.20 Hay 6
Buster ....3.15 Kem 6

C

Cadford Balerina 4.45 Str 6
Caerdydd (IRE) 3.15 Kem 7
Calachuchi ....2.15 Hay 2
Call At Eight (USA) ....3.30 Sou 7
Call For Rooney 5.00 Thi 4
Call Racecall ....2.00 Thi 3
Campal.............4.30 Sou 4
Canbrack Style ..2.30 Thi 6
Cannon's Spirit..4.00 Sou 6
Canny Chronicle 4.00 Thi 4
Canoness.........4.45 Kem 6
Capability Brown 2.00 Thi 4
Cape Pigeon (USA) ....3.45 Kem 5
Caraball Dancer 5.00 Thi 5
Carole's King (IRE) ....4.00 Thi 5
Carpet Slippers 4.45 Kem 7
Cashtal Dazzler 3.50 Hay 4
Castle Maid....2.15 Kem 4
Castoret..........3.45 Kem 6
Caveat Vendor..5.00 Thi 6
Ceciliano (USA) 1.45 Hay 2
Cedrela (USA) ...4.00 Thi 6
Celestial Sky....3.30 Sou 8
Cellatica (USA) 4.30 Sou 5
Cellatica (USA) 5.00 Sou 8
Charcoal Burner 5.15 Kem 10
Charden..........4.45 Kem 8
Charlafrivola...3.20 Hay 2
Charlafrivola....4.00 Thi 7
Charlycia..........3.00 Sou 6
Charly Pharly (FR) ....5.00 Sou 9
Charly Pharly (FR) ....3.00 Thi 5
Chateau de Berne (USA) ....2.30 Sou 8
Chiefs Kraal (NZ) 4.45 Str 7
Childrey (USA)...2.30 Thi 7
Choir Leader...2.45 Kem 9
Choir Leader ....2.30 Thi 8
Ciboure ....4.20 Hay 7
Clare Court.....4.45 Kem 9
Claret (IRE).....3.20 Hay 3
Classic Ring (IRE) ....3.00 Sou 7
Classic Statement 1.45 Hay 3
Claudia Miss.....2.30 Thi 9
Clean Up..........3.00 Sou 8
Clear Call (FR)...4.15 Str 3
Clouded Lamp (USA) ....5.15 Kem 11
Colorfayre.......3.30 Sou 9
Colour Scheme..2.30 Sou 9
Colour Scheme 5.00 Sou 10
Colway Ann......4.00 Thi 8
Comedie Fleur...4.30 Thi 7
Comedy River ..2.30 Thi 10
Coney Island ....3.00 Sou 9
Contractors Dream ....3.30 Sou 10
Cool Calculator 3.30 Sou 11
Cool Run.........2.15 Hay 3
Corcina ....4.00 Thi 9
Cormorant Creek 5.15 Kem 12
Corrin Hill.......4.00 Sou 7
Courting Newmarket ....3.30 Sou 12
Court Rapier.....3.15 Str 2
Crail Harbour ...4.00 Sou 8
Crazy River .....4.45 Str 8
Crystal Heights (FR) ....3.30 Sou 13
Crystal Spirit....1.45 Hay 4
Cut The Music (IRE) ....5.00 Thi 7

D

Daily Sport Soon 3.45 Str 7
Daily Sport Soon 5.15 Str 8
Del Miss ....2.30 Thi 11
Damanour (USA) 3.45 Str 8
Dancing Breeze 2.30 Sou 10
Dancing Days...3.00 Thi 6
Daragency.......3.00 Sou 10
Darlin' Again....3.45 Str 9
Darussalam......3.30 Thi 2
Dashing Fellow (IRE) ....3.30 Sou 14
Dauntess ....3.15 Kem 5
Dayjur (USA)... 2.45 Hay 1
Daymer Bay.....4.30 Sou 6
Dead Certain...2.45 Hay 2
Dear Old Girl...2.30 Sou 11
Debach Daisy. 2.45 Kem 10
Debach Daisy...2.30 Thi 12
Deb's Ball ....3.00 Thi 7
Deep Impression 4.15 Str 4
Dellwood Renown ....5.15 Kem 13
Derby Cup (USA) 3.00 Sou 11
Derby Cup (USA) 4.00 Thi 10
Derechef.......2.45 Kem 11
Designer Stubble 4.20 Hay 8
Desire's Double 4.00 Thi 11
Detour (IRE) ...3.30 Sou 15
Diamond Inthe Dark (USA)...........3.30 Sou 16
Diamond Wind (USA) ....3.00 Sou 12
Dick Knight.....3.45 Str 10
Distinct Native 4.45 Kem 10
Doire ....3.30 Sou 17
Dokkha Oyston (IRE) ....4.20 Hay 9
Dollar Seeker (USA) ....5.00 Sou 11
Double Entendre 3.45 Kem 7
Dovale ....4.20 Hay 10
Dovale..........4.00 Thi 12
Dr Bill............3.30 Sou 18
Dreaming Spires 2.30 Sou 12
Drinks Party (IRE) ....3.00 Sou 13
Drinks Party (IRE) ....4.00 Thi 13
Drmanum.........5.00 Thi 8
Dublin Breeze ..5.00 Sou 12
Duck And Dive 2.45 Hay 3
Dulcimal (IRE) 3.30 Sou 19
Dust Devil ......3.50 Hay 5
Dutch Angel ...3.30 Sou 20
Dynamic Quest ..4.45 Str 9
Dzet (USA)......4.45 Str 10

E

Eastern Music..4.20 Hay 11
Easy Over (USA) 5.15 Str 4
Eckly (IRE).....3.00 Sou 14
El Arab ....4.50 Hay 4
Ela-Yemou ....4.45 Str 11
El Capistrano ....5.15 Str 5
Electric Dancer. 3.45 Str 11
Elegant Pearl....4.30 Sou 7
Elmajarrah (CAN) ....2.45 Kem 12
Elwadi ....4.45 Str 12
Emerald Sunset 3.45 Str 12
Enterprise Lady (FR) ....5.15 Kem 14
Eradicate ....3.50 Hay 6
Erin's Town.....3.00 Thi 8
Erostin Floats...4.15 Str 6
Escape Talk.....3.00 Thi 9
Euro Galaxy....2.30 Thi 13
Ever Reckless...3.45 Str 13
Execution Only (IRE) ....4.00 Thi 14
Express Account 2.45 Kem 13
Express Account 5.15 Kem 15

F

Fact Finder....3.45 Kem 8
Factotum ....5.15 Str 6
Falland...........4.45 Str 13
Family At War (USA) ....4.30 Thi 8
Famous Run.....2.45 Str 2
Farlsi (USA).....3.20 Hay 4
Fascinating Lady 3.00 Sou 15
Fast And Free...3.45 Str 14
Fast-Talkin Tinker (IRE) ....3.20 Hay 5
Fearsome ....3.45 Str 15
Fermentation (IRE) ....3.00 Sou 16
Fiery Sun ....1.45 Hay 5
Fight Again ....3.45 Str 16
Final Deed ......3.20 Hay 6
Final Offer (USA) 3.15 Kem 8
Fingers Crossed ..5.15 Str 7
Finlux Sky Design ....3.30 Sou 13
Fire Top ....3.50 Hay 7
First Avenue...5.15 Kem 16
First Exhibition 4.45 Str 14
First Home.....5.00 Sou 13
Florida Gold ...2.30 Sou 14
Flown...........4.45 Kem 11
Fluent In Spanish 3.30 Sou 21
Fluorescent Flo 2.30 Thi 14
Folk Dance.......4.15 Str 6
Follow The Sea 5.15 Kem 17
Foot Stick........4.15 Str 7

For Real .... 3.30 Thi 3
Fouringh........ 4.00 Thi 15
Fox Chapel.... 3.45 Kem 9
Fragrant Park .. 2.00 Thi 5
French House.. 2.30 Thi 15
French Senor (USA) .... 3.45 Kem 10
Frendly Fellow .. 5.15 Str 8
Friday Fourball 3.00 Sou 17
Full Strength .... 3.15 Str 3
Full Strength .... 4.15 Str 8
Funun (USA) .. 2.45 Kem 14
Future Glory.... 3.00 Thi 10

G

Gaelic Chief .... 4.20 Hay 12
Gaelic Dancer . 2.30 Sou 15
Galagames (USA) 4.20 Sou 8
Galaxy Glow ... 3.00 Sou 16
Gallery Artist (IRE) .... 3.30 Sou 22
Garth Lady.... 4.45 Kem 12
Gavin Allen ... 3.30 Sou 23
Gay Revenge.. 3.30 Sou 24
Gembridge Jupiter 4.15 Str 9
Gemini Fire...... 3.30 Thi 4
Generous (IRE) 3.20 Hay 7
Genotin........ 3.45 Kem 11
Gentle Gain .. 2.45 Kem 15
Ghilan (USA)... 3.45 Str 17
Gibbot.......... 5.15 Kem 18
Gilt Premium ... 4.45 Str 15
Gipsy King...... 4.20 Hay 13
Givemeacall .... 3.00 Sou 19
Glastondale..... 3.00 Thi 11
Glazerite .... 1.45 Hay 6
Glebelands Girl 4.45 Str 16
Glenstal Princess 4.00 Sou 9
God Bless You . 3.50 Hay 8
Godly Light (FR) 4.00 Sou 10
Golden Beau . 3.45 Kem 13
Golden Delia . 2.45 Kem 17
Golden Gunner (IRE) .... 3.30 Sou 25
Golden Isle..... 5.00 Sou 14
Golden Vintage 5.00 Sou 15
Gold Nostalgia 2.45 Kem 16
Gold Prospect... 4.50 Hay 5
Gold Prospect 3.45 Kem 12
Goldstream (USA) 3.00 Thi 12
Goodfellows Lot 3.30 Thi 5
Go Pathfinder 5.15 Kem 19
Gracewing ...... 2.30 Thi 16
Gran Alba (USA) 3.50 Hay 9
Granitton Bay .. 4.50 Hay 6
Great Commotion (USA) .... 2.45 Hay 4
Great Gusto.... 5.00 Sou 16
Great Service.. 5.00 Sou 17
Great Star ...... 5.00 Thi 9
Green Lane (USA) .... 3.20 Hay 8
Green Tin Hut (USA) .... 4.30 Sou 9
Grey Area...... 2.30 Thi 17
Grey Commander 3.00 Sou 20
Grey Earl....... 3.00 Sou 21
Grey North..... 3.00 Sou 22
Grey Realm .... 3.00 Sou 23
Grey Tudor ..... 4.45 Str 17
Grondola........ 4.45 Str 18
Greve Aries (IRE) .... 4.20 Hay 14
Greve Aries (IRE) .... 3.15 Kem 9
Grown At Rowan .... 2.45 Kem 18
Guidobaldo (USA) 3.00 Thi 13
Gunboat....... 3.45 Kem 14
Gymcrak Gamble 3.00 Sou 24
Gypsy River (USA) .... 3.45 Kem 15

H

Hackforth .... 4.50 Hay 7
Halkopous..... 4.45 Kem 13
Hardiheroine .... 4.45 Str 19
Harvest Minstrel 2.30 Sou 16
Hawwam ...... 3.45 Kem 16
Headrest .... 4.30 Sou 10
Heard A Whisper 3.15 Kem 10
Heaven-Liegh-Grey .... 4.30 Thi 9
Hello My Darling (IRE) .... 3.20 Hay 9
Henri Le Comte 4.45 Str 20
Here He Comes 5.15 Kem 20
Hickory Wind .. 2.30 Thi 18
Highland Spirit 4.00 Thi 18
Hills Of Hoy ... 5.15 Kem 21
Hinari Video .... 4.00 Sou 11
Hiram B Birdbath 5.15 Str 9
Hold Court (IRE) 5.00 Thi 10
Homestead Lad 3.00 Sou 25
Hot Rumour..... 1.45 Hay 7
Housatonic (USA) 5.00 Sou 18
Husyan (USA) .. 4.15 Kem 2
Hydeonius ..... 3.00 Thi 14
Hydropic ...... 2.30 Sou 17

I

Ibn Sina (USA) 5.15 Kem 22
Ice Magic .... 3.00 Thi 15
Ile de Nisky.... 4.15 Kem 3
Illogical......... 4.30 Sou 11
Imaginary Plane 5.00 Thi 11
Inaad........... 3.50 Hay 10
Inbihar .... 2.45 Kem 19
Inbihar .... 5.15 Kem 23
Indian Maestro 3.45 Kem 17
Indian Maestro 4.00 Sou 12
Indian Queen... 4.15 Kem 4
In Truth .... 5.00 Thi 12
Irish Emerald.. 3.50 Hay 11
Island Jetsetter. 5.15 Str 10
It's The Pits ... 4.45 Kem 14
Ittisaal .... 2.15 Kem 6
Ivoroski......... 3.00 Thi 16
Ivory Way (USA) 4.45 Kem 15

J

Jack Boy .... 3.30 Thi 6
Jahafil .... 3.20 Hay 10
Jallad (USA) .. 3.15 Kem 11
J Brand .... 4.45 Kem 16
Jenufa (IRE) ... 4.20 Hay 15
Jimlil .... 3.30 Sou 26
John O'Dee...... 4.15 Str 10
Jois de Rose .... 4.50 Hay 8
Jois de Rose... 3.45 Kem 18
Jolizal .... 4.00 Thi 17
Jolly Fisherman (IRE) .... 3.00 Sou 26
Jomana .... 3.45 Str 18
Jonbel......... 3.00 Sou 27
Just A Look.... 3.30 Sou 27
Just A Step..... 4.00 Sou 13
Just Jennings .. 4.00 Sou 14
Just Ready (IRE) 5.00 Thi 13

K

Kabcast .... 3.30 Thi 7
Kagram Queen 4.00 Thi 18
Kalalee.......... 4.45 Str 21
Kalmadene .... 4.45 Kem 17
Kandara (FR) .. 4.20 Hay 16
Kariba Dam .... 5.00 Thi 14
Karnatak......... 3.15 Str 4
Karnatak......... 4.15 Str 11
Kashmir Gold.. 3.00 Sou 28
Kawtuban...... 3.50 Hay 12
Keen Melody (USA) .... 2.45 Kem 20
Keep Your Word 5.15 Kem 24
Kevinsbelle ..... 4.00 Thi 19
Khaydara .... 4.50 Hay 9
Khios (USA) .... 4.45 Str 22
Kibreet......... 3.45 Kem 19
King High ...... 1.45 Hay 8
King Noddy .... 3.00 Sou 29
Kiralyi (FR) .... 4.30 Sou 12
Kiwi Tauka (NZ) 3.45 Str 19
Knave Of Clubs. 2.00 Thi 6
Knight Of Kirkton 4.45 Str 23
Knockennis...... 5.15 Str 11
Knowsfence..... 3.45 Str 20
Kohinoor (IRE) 3.20 Hay 11
Kolinsky .... 5.00 Sou 19
Kolinsky........ 3.00 Thi 17
Kreischim (IRE) 3.30 Sou 28

L

Lady Jemma (IRE) .... 3.00 Sou 30
Lady Lacey ..... 2.15 Kem 8
Lady Lacey .... 2.45 Kem 21
Lady Scothald (IRE) .... 3.30 Sou 29
Lady Vixen (USA) .... 2.45 Kem 22
Lafkadio........ 2.30 Sou 18
La Masnas (USA) 4.30 Thi 10
Land Of Hope 2.45 Kem 23
Langtry Lady 3.45 Kem 20
La Stupenda .. 2.15 Kem 7
La Visir (USA).. 1.45 Hay 9
Le Bambino ...... 3.15 Str 5
Left Right ...... 4.00 Sou 15
Left Right .... 3.30 Thi 8
Legal Case...... 4.15 Kem 5
Legal Tina ...... 3.45 Str 21
Legal Tina ...... 5.15 Str 12
Le Passe Temps 4.30 Sou 13
Level Xing ..... 4.20 Hay 17
Light Dancer .... 2.15 Str 1
Light Dancer ... 5.15 Str 13
Light Hand ... 5.15 Kem 25
Like Amber ...... 3.30 Thi 9
Lilac Time ..... 5.00 Sou 20
Lincstone Boy (IRE) .... 4.30 Thi 11
Lisa Rosa .... 2.00 Thi 7
Local Dealer ... 5.00 Thi 15
Loco Tycoon.... 3.00 Thi 18
Lofty Lady (IRE) 3.20 Hay 12
Logical Lady . 2.45 Kem 24
Longwood Legend .... 3.30 Sou 30
Lord David S (USA) .... 3.50 Hay 13
Lord Of The Field .... 4.15 Kem 6
Love Forty ..... 4.30 Sou 14
Loyalty (IRE)... 3.00 Sou 31
Lugana Beach.. 2.45 Hay 5
Lusum .... 4.50 Hay 10
Lynseys Lad .... 4.45 Str 24

M

Macconachie..... 3.00 Thi 8
Mac Kelty ...... 2.30 Sou 19
Magic Secret.... 5.00 Thi 16
Magnetism .... 2.45 Kem 25
Mahrajan....... 4.45 Kem 18
Maid Of Essex .. 3.00 Thi 19
Main Fleet...... 4.30 Sou 15
Mai Pen Rai .... 4.00 Thi 20
Mallood (USA) 3.15 Kem 12
Make Contact (USA) .... 1.45 Hay 10
Manchesterskytrain .... 5.15 Kem 26
Mantraki .... 3.45 Kem 21
Maple Hayes ... 3.45 Str 22
Maple Walk ..... 4.45 Str 25
Maraakis (USA) 3.20 Hay 13
Marastib (IRE). 4.30 Thi 12
Marching Past 4.20 Hay 18
Marching Past. 3.30 Sou 31
Mardessa .... 5.00 Thi 17
Margs Girl ..... 2.30 Sou 20
Marqub (USA) .. 2.15 Hay 4
Mashhor John .. 5.00 Thi 18
Masked Ball..... 2.15 Hay 5
Master Line ... 4.45 Kem 19
Master Pierre.. 5.15 Kem 27
Master Plan (FR) 2.15 Hay 6
Master Vince ..... 3.15 Str 6
Matador (USA) 4.45 Kem 20
Mazatlan......... 5.00 Thi 19
MCA Below The Line .... 4.00 Thi 23
Meeson Code ... 5.00 Sou 21
Meeson Code .... 2.00 Thi 9
Meeson Code ... 3.00 Thi 20
Melancolia ..... 3.50 Hay 14
Meldon Song ... 4.20 Hay 19
Mel's Rose .... 3.45 Kem 22
Merchant Of Venice .... 5.00 Thi 20
Merpet .... 3.00 Sou 32
Mexican Vision 3.45 Kem 23
Miad............ 2.30 Thi 19
Milclere .... 3.45 Str 23
Millpond Boy .. 4.45 Kem 21
Mimi's Machine 3.00 Sou 33
Minizen Music (IRE) .... 4.20 Hay 20
Miss Appropriate 3.00 Sou 34
Miss Calculate .. 4.00 Thi 21
Mississippi Beat (USA) .... 4.20 Sou 16
Mississippi Beat (USA) .... 2.00 Thi 10
Miss Kellybell.. 4.00 Sou 16
Miss Kellybell .. 3.30 Thi 10
Miss Knight .... 4.00 Sou 17
Miss Reisun .... 5.00 Sou 22
Mister Feathers 4.15 Str 12
Mister Tuftie.... 3.45 Str 24
Mistral's Dancer 2.30 Sou 21
Mistress Carroll 2.30 Sou 22
Misty Eyes ..... 5.00 Sou 23
Misty Goddess (IRE) .... 5.00 Thi 21
Misty Night..... 5.00 Thi 22
Model Child .... 3.30 Sou 32
Model Nurse.... 2.30 Sou 23
Mohawk Chief (IRE) .... 3.15 Kem 13
Molly Splash .. 2.45 Kem 26
Momentsofmusic 4.00 Thi 22
Montpelier Lad 3.45 Kem 24
Montykosky..... 2.00 Thi 11
Moon Reef ..... 5.00 Sou 24
Morpick .... 4.00 Sou 18
Mossy Rose..... 4.00 Sou 19
Mostimus ...... 4.20 Hay 21
Motcombs....... 4.45 Str 26
Mr Kirby......... 3.45 Str 3
Mr Reiner (IRE) 5.00 Thi 23
Mujaazif (USA) 5.00 Thi 24
Murango .... 4.45 Kem 22
Murphy.......... 5.15 Str 14
My Diamond Ring .... 3.45 Kem 25
My Lord (USA) 3.50 Hay 15
My Lucky Lady 3.00 Sou 35
My Opinion ..... 3.00 Thi 21
Mystic Bid ..... 2.30 Sou 24

N

Nafsawa (USA). 1.45 Hay 11
Nal Harn........ 4.00 Thi 24
Nangarar (USA) 3.50 Hay 16
Native Tribe.... 3.50 Hay 17
Nearly Ready..... 3.15 Str 7
Nearroe......... 5.15 Kem 28
Needwood Sprite 2.15 Hay 7
Needwood Sprite 5.15 Kem 29
Neenawn ...... 5.15 Kem 30
Neverdown .... 2.45 Kem 27
New Outlook..... 2.45 Str 4
Nightmare Knave 4.00 Sou 20
Ninety-Nine (IRE) 5.00 Thi 25
Nipotina........ 3.00 Thi 22
Nishkina .... 3.00 Sou 36
Noble Son...... 5.00 Sou 25
No Decision .... 2.30 Sou 25
Nodolya .... 2.30 Sou 26
Nonstop .... 3.15 Str 8
Norstock ...... 2.45 Kem 28
Northants .... 2.15 Hay 8
North Base ..... 2.30 Sou 27
Northern Habit 3.45 Kem 26
Northern Rocket 4.00 Sou 21
Northern Spark 4.20 Hay 22

Northern Village 5.00 Sou 26
Northgate King 5.15 Kem 31
North Of Watford 3.30 Thi 11

O

Obolov.........3.30 Thi 12
Observation Post 4.15 Kem 7
Occamist (USA) . 2.15 Str 2
Ocean Air......3.20 Hay 14
Old Mother Goose
...............5.00 Sou 27
Olivers Mount (USA)
...............3.20 Hay 15
One For The Chief 5.00 Thi 26
On Strike (IRE) 4.00 Thi 25
Oratel Flyer....4.00 Sea 22
Oratel Flyer....2.20 Thi 12
Orchard's Pet ..4.00 Sou 23
Orleans Girl....3.15 Kem 9
Orleans Girl...2.45 Kem 29
Or Nor ....2.30 Sou 28
Ostura ....4.45 Kem 23
Our Fan.........4.00 Sou 24
Overpower.....5.15 Kem 32
Oxbow ....4.30 Sou 17

P

Palm House.....5.15 Str 15
Panama Pete (IRE)
...............4.00 Thi 26
Panacong........5.00 Sou 26
Paper Craft.....5.00 Sou 29
Paper Dart (USA)
...............3.15 Kem 14
Paper Shoes ....3.30 Thi 14
Paradigm's Vision (IRE)
...............3.00 Sou 37
Parking Bay...5.15 Kem 33
Passed Pawn...5.00 Sou 30
Pattie's Grey...4.00 Sou 25
Pecking Order . 3.45 Str 25
Pedantry (IRE) 3.00 Sou 38
Pelagian Zest...3.00 Thi 23
Perfect Prince (IRE)
...............3.00 Sou 39
Persian House 4.45 Kem 24
Persian Lord ..5.15 Kem 34
Perspicacity...2.45 Kem 30
Persuasive .....3.50 Hay 18
Phalarope (IRE) 4.00 Thi 27
Pharaoh's Delight
...............2.45 Hay 6
Pharmopi......2.45 Kem 31
Phil-Blake ......4.45 Str 27
Philipintown Lad 2.45 Str 5
Philosophos ....1.45 Hay 12
Pick And Choose 3.30 Sou 33
Pic Negre.......2.30 Sou 29
Pier Damiani (USA)
...............4.15 Kem 8
Pigalle Wonder 4.20 Hay 23
Pinemartin.......2.45 Str 6
Pine Ridge Lady 4.45 Str 28
Pintail Bay .....3.00 Thi 24
Pleasant Company
...............4.30 Sou 18
Plie............2.45 Kem 32
Polly Muldowney
...............2.45 Kem 33
Popthorn.........3.15 Str 9
Porridge Oats...3.45 Str 26
Portofino......5.15 Kem 35
Portofino.......5.00 Sea 31
Postage Stamp 4.45 Kem 25
Premier Dance 2.30 Sou 30
Premier Touch 4.50 Hay 11
President George 2.30 Sou 31
Pressure Game . 5.15 Str 16
Pretonic........3.30 Sou 34
Prince Ibrahim 3.45 Kem 27
Prince Klenk.....2.45 Str 7
Prince Sobur ...1.45 Hay 13
Princess Roxanne 2.30 Sea 22
Princess Roxanne 4.30 Sea 19
Prior Charge ...2.30 Sou 33
Priory Bay ......3.45 Str 27
Prix Du Nord (USA)
...............2.15 Str 3
Profit A Prendre 3.45 Kem 28
Pussy Foot......3.30 Thi 15

Q

Quagilino (USA) 3.20 Hay 16
Qualitair Dream 4.50 Hay 12
Qualitair Melody 3.00 Sou 40
Quatre Femme 2.15 Kem 10
Quick Tempo ...4.45 Str 29
Quiet Achiever (CAN)
...............5.15 Kem 36
Quiet Riot ......3.45 Str 28
Quinta (IRE) ...3.00 Sou 41
Quip...........4.45 Kem 26
Quip...........3.00 Thi 25

R

Radio Caroline 4.00 Thi 28
Ragtime ....3.00 Thi 26
Rah Wan (USA) 5.15 Kem 37
Rainbow Stripes 2.00 Thi 12
Rambo Express 4.00 Sou 26
Rathbrides Joy 2.00 Thi 13
Real Stunner ..2.15 Kem 11
Red Rainbow...5.00 Thi 27
Red Rosein.....4.00 Sea 27
Red Rosein .....3.30 Thi 16
Reklaw ....3.00 Thi 27
Retouch ....1.45 Hay 14
Reza ....3.30 Sou 35
Riffs Park.......3.00 Sou 42
Right Step (FR) 3.00 Thi 28
Ringtop (USA). 2.30 Thi 20
Rio Piedras......2.15 Hay 9
Riva's Touch (USA)
...............3.15 Str 10
Robellation (USA)
...............4.50 Hay 13
Robins Return 3.30 Sou 36
Rodeo Star (USA) 3.00 Thi 29
Rolfeson........3.45 Kem 29
Roman Walk...2.15 Kem 12
Ron's Victory (USA)
...............2.45 Hay 7
Roosters Tipple 4.00 Sou 28
Roseate Lodge 3.45 Kem 30
Roseate Tern...4.15 Kem 9
Roses Have Thorns
...............2.45 Kem 34
Rossmichael ....3.45 Str 29
Rosy Diamond 3.45 Kem 31
Rousillon To Be 4.30 Sea 20
Rousillon To Be 2.00 Thi 14
Rouski ....4.00 Sou 29
Routilante.....2.15 Kem 13
Rowhedge........2.15 Str 4
Royal Academy (USA)
...............2.45 Hay 8
Royal Dartmouth (USA)
...............3.45 Kem 32
Royal Fan ......3.30 Thi 17
Royal Girl ....2.30 Thi 21
Royal Hunt .....3.45 Str 30
Royal Passion 2.45 Kem 35
Ruby Shoes ...5.00 Sou 32
Rudda Cass....3.00 Thi 30
Rudry Princess 2.30 Sou 34
Rue de Fort ....5.00 Thi 28
Rue Du Cirque (IRE)
...............4.00 Thi 29
Ruiz Miguel ...5.15 Kem 38
Runcible Cat (USA)
...............3.45 Str 31
Runway Romance (FR)
...............4.45 Str 30
Ryedale Lass...3.00 Sou 43

S

Sabonis (USA). 2.30 Sou 35
Sacosha ....3.30 Sou 36
Safety (USA) ....4.45 Str 31
Sagacious Lady (USA)
...............4.45 Str 32
Sailor's Delight ..2.45 Str 8
Sail Past (FR)..4.20 Hay 24
Saint Bene't (IRE) 4.00 Thi 30
Saint Bene't (IRE) 5.00 Thi 29
Sakura Dancer 2.30 Sou 37
Sally's Prince (IRE)
...............2.30 Sea 37
Sally's Prince (IRE)
...............4.00 Thi 31
Sallys Won ....5.15 Kem 39
Sandsumo ....4.45 Str 33
Sans Frais.......3.30 Sou 38
Sapphirine ....5.15 Kem 40
Sapphirine.....2.30 Sea 38
Sarah Carter.....4.45 Str 34
Sarsta Grai ......4.00 Thi 32
Satin Lake (USA) 5.00 Sou 33
Sawaki.........2.45 Kem 36
Sayalot............2.15 Str 5
Say A Prayer...2.30 Sea 39
Say A Prayer...5.00 Sea 34
Scarlet Express 2.00 Thi 15
Scatter..........4.50 Hay 14
Scotoni ....5.15 Kem 41
Sea Of Love ....4.00 Thi 33
Secret Hase.....4.00 Thi 34
Serenoski .....3.00 Sou 44
Sexton Boy.......2.15 Str 6
Shadowland (IRE)
...............3.30 Sou 39
Shady Pimpernel 5.00 Thi 30
Shalford (IRE) 3.15 Kem 15
Shannon Express
...............5.15 Kem 42
Sharp Glow ....3.00 Sou 45
Sharp Runner (FR)
...............4.00 Sou 30
Sharp To Oblige 2.30 Thi 22
Sheer Precocity 4.50 Hay 15
Sherjamal (USA) 2.30 Thi 23
She's Smart.....4.20 Hay 25
Shesnice (IRE) 3.15 Kem 16
Shimmering Scarlet (IRE)
...............5.00 Thi 31
Shining Jewel...2.30 Thi 24
Short Straw ...5.15 Kem 43
Shout Fore......4.00 Sou 31
Shout Out ......2.30 Thi 25
Siberian Breeze 3.30 Sou 40
Sibton Abbey ....2.45 Str 9
Silken Sailed (USA)
...............4.30 Thi 13
Silver Owl.....4.45 Kem 27
Simply Des.....5.15 Kem 44
Singing Flame...2.45 Str 10
Singing Gold ..5.15 Kem 45
Singing Star ....3.30 Thi 18
Single ....3.45 Kem 33
Sing Out (FR)..3.30 Sou 41
Sir Nick..........4.45 Str 35
Sir Peter Lely...2.00 Thi 16
Sister Sal.......2.45 Kem 37
Skisurf ....1.45 Hay 15
Sky Drama......3.30 Sou 42
Sky Venture.....2.45 Str 11
Slades Hill ....3.30 Thi 19
Sleepline Palace 2.30 Sou 40
Slick Cherry...5.15 Kem 46
Sloe Berry.......3.30 Thi 20
Small Double (IRE)
...............3.30 Sou 43
Smart Magician (USA)
...............5.00 Sea 35
Smart Magician (USA)
...............2.00 Thi 31
Smiles Ahead...5.00 Thi 32
Smuggle ....4.50 Hay 16
Smuggle ....2.45 Kem 38
So Apt (IRE)...3.30 Sou 44
Solde...........3.20 Hay 17
Soleil Grand ...4.50 Hay 17
Solid (IRE).....3.30 Sou 45
Song Of Sixpence (USA)
...............4.15 Kem 10
Sonsie Lad .....3.30 Sou 46
Souter's Hill (USA)
...............4.30 Sou 21
Spanish Harlem 3.30 Thi 21
Spanish Love. 5.15 Kem 47
Spanish Realm 2.45 Kem 39
Spar Lady........3.45 Str 32
Spearman......3.50 Hay 19
Spearman .....4.45 Kem 28
Spinechiller.....4.30 Thi 14
Spitzabit ....4.00 Sou 32
Spring Wedding 3.45 Str 33
Spritsail ....4.15 Kem 11
Squadron (CAN) 5.15 Str 17
Starchy Blake...3.45 Str 34
Stately March . 3.30 Sou 47
Statoblest.......2.45 Hay 9
Stella Bianca (USA)
...............4.45 Kem 29
Steven John ....2.00 Thi 17
St Louis Blues...5.15 Str 18
Stocktina......2.15 Kem 14
Stone Flake (USA)
...............4.45 Kem 30
Stone Madness...2.15 Str 7
Storm At Night (USA)
...............3.15 Kem 18
Stormy Belle ..2.15 Kem 15
St Patrick's Day 3.15 Kem 17
Streckinski .....5.00 Thi 33
Strip Cartoon (IRE)
...............4.00 Thi 35
Strong Approach 2.45 Str 12
Stuffy (IRE).....5.00 Thi 34
Sugemar.......4.45 Kem 31
Sunday Sport's Pet
...............2.30 Sou 41
Sunset And Vine 4.30 Sou 23
Sunset Rose ....3.00 Thi 32
Supadupa.....2.45 Kem 40
Superendo .....3.00 Sou 46
Super Sally....2.15 Kem 16
Super Sally.....2.30 Thi 28
Surzas ....4.45 Str 36
Sweet Bay......5.15 Kem 48
Swingaway Lady 4.20 Hay 26
Swingtime Belle 4.45 Str 37
Sword Excalibur 4.30 Sea 23
Sword Excalibur 2.00 Thi 18
Sylvan Breeze 3.15 Kem 19
Sylvan Tempest 4.45 Kem 32

T

Tabyan (USA) 2.15 Kem 17
Tara's Delight 5.15 Kem 49
Tarda ....2.30 Sou 42
Tartan Tinker (IRE)
...............5.00 Thi 36
Tartan Trademark 4.15 Str 13
Taylor's Realm 5.15 Kem 50
Telegraphier (IRE)
...............3.00 Sou 47
Tesekkurederim 2.00 Thi 19
Thar-An-Bharr...3.15 Str 11
The Groovy Kipper
...............3.00 Sou 48
The Healy ......2.00 Thi 20
The Jones Boy (FR)
...............3.45 Kem 34
The Mague .....3.00 Thi 33
The Prodigal...5.15 Kem 51
The Shanahan Bay
...............4.00 Sou 33
The Singing Man 3.30 Thi 22
Thoresby.......2.30 Sou 43
Thorn Goddess (IRE)
...............3.30 Sou 48
Thorny Flat (IRE)
...............4.20 Hay 27
Thunderball ....2.30 Thi 27
Thurlestone (NZ) 2.45 Str 13
Tiger Cub (USA) 5.15 Kem 52
Timbilyn (IRE) 4.00 Thi 36
Time For The Blues (IRE)
...............4.20 Hay 28
Time Gentlemen 3.15 Kem 20
Timeless Times (USA)
...............3.15 Kem 21

Timeless Times (USA) ....4.30 Thi 15
Time Of My Life 3.00 Bou 40
Time's Angel ....4.45 Str 38
Timea (USA)....3.50 Hay 30
Timea (USA)....4.45 Kem 33
Tiswa (USA)....3.15 Kem 22
Toby Henry.....5.00 Thi 36
Tod ....2.45 Hay 10
Tom Rum ......5.15 Kem 53
Tom's Prospect (USA) ....3.00 Bou 50
Too Much Champagne (IRE) ....4.00 Thi 37
Top Of The Bill 5.00 Sou 36
Top Of The Bill 2.00 Thi 21
Top One.........3.45 Kem 35
Top Tern.........3.00 Bou 51
Torghia...........5.15 Kem 54
To-Severals (IRE) 3.30 Bou 40
Toushtari (USA) 2.15 Hay 10
Travelling Tryst (USA) ....4.45 Kem 34
Travelling Tryst (USA) ....3.00 Thi 34
Travel Noon....3.00 Bou 52
Treasy Stone Lady ....3.00 Sou 53
Treasy Stone Lady ....5.00 Thi 37
Tribal Mascot (USA) ....5.15 Str 19

Tristiorum.......2.30 Thi 28
Trojan Excel...2.30 Bou 44
Tropico ....3.45 Str 35
Tudor D'Or .....3.45 Str 36
Turks Head Ten 3.30 Bou 50
Tusky.............4.20 Hay 29
Two Badges (IRE) ....3.30 Bou 51
Tyrian ....2.15 Hay 11
Tyrian Purple (IRE) ....5.00 Thi 38
Tyrnippy ....5.00 Bou 37

U

Ullswater.........3.45 Str 37
Upham Rainbow 2.45 Str 14

W

Vague Shot.....4.50 Hay 18
Vaig Appeal...3.45 Kem 36
Vain Prince.....2.00 Thi 22
Valiant Saint...4.00 Bou 34
Valldemosa.....3.30 Thi 23
Valtaki ....5.15 Str 20
Vanroy ....3.45 Kem 37
Vestige ....2.00 Thi 23
Viking Lady....3.00 Bou 54
Vinegar Bob....4.30 Bou 24
Vintage..........4.45 Kem 35
Visage............2.15 Hay 12
Volcalmeh......3.30 Bou 53
Walking Saint 2.45 Kem 41
Waltzing Home 2.30 Bou 45
Wanda's Dream (USA) ....3.15 Kem 23

Water God ....4.45 Kem 36
Watermeet Down 4.15 Str 14
Wave Master....4.45 Str 39
Wayward Singer 2.45 Str 15
Welsh Oak........4.15 Str 15
Western Dynasty 4.45 Kem 37
Western Secret 2.00 Thi 24
Western Wolf..3.45 Kem 38
Westmead.......3.45 Str 38
What A Card ...3.00 Bou 55
Where's Carol ..3.00 Bou 56
Who's Tef (IRE) 4.20 Hay 30
Will He Or Wont He (IRE) ....3.30 Bou 53
William Anthony 2.45 Str 16
Wimborne ......5.00 Bou 38
Windward Ariom 3.00 Thi 35
Winters Hill .....2.45 Str 17
Wise Cracker ....4.15 Str 16
Wishlon (USA). 5.00 Bou 39
Witness Box (USA) ....3.50 Hay 21
Wolfgang ....2.00 Thi 25
Wolf Hall (IRE) 4.30 Thi 16
Wolver Gold ....4.45 Str 40
Woodlands Lady 3.45 Str 39
World's Creation (USA) ....4.00 Thi 38
Wrybill ....4.50 Hay 19

XYZ

Xai-Tang ....5.15 Kem 56
Yajib (USA) ....1.45 Hay 16
Yankee Flyer. 2.45 Kem 42
Yearsley ....4.50 Hay 20
Yellow Bear....4.00 Bou 35
Yes.................4.20 Hay 31
You Are A Star 3.45 Kem 39
You Know The Rules ....2.45 Kem 43
You Know The Rules ....4.45 Kem 38
Young Pact.....2.15 Hay 13
Young Jam.....3.45 Kem 40
Zamboanga ....5.00 Sou 40
Zamboanga.....3.00 Thi 36
Zandril ....3.15 Kem 34
Zinger............3.00 Bou 57
Zizi Jean Maire 2.30 Thi 29
Zolly's Treasure 3.30 Bou 54

STRATFORD SATURDAY

ADVANCE GOING: Good to Firm

2.15 Black Prince Conditional Jockeys' Selling Handicap Hurdle 2¾m

£2000 added to stakes for 4,5 & 6-y-o only £20 to enter Lowest weight 10st 7lb Pen, after Sept 1st, a winner of a hurdle 6lb To be ridden by Conditional Jockeys Allowances: Riders who have not ridden 5 winners 7lb (Flat races, Apprentice races and Conditional Jockeys races included) The winner to be sold by auction in accordance with the Rules of Racing for £2000 Minimum Claiming Price of any other horse starting £4000 Closed on Sept 3

TOPWEIGHT OFFICIALLY RATED 86

Form	Horse (Owner)	Trainer	Age-Wt	OR	SW	
004-1	Rowhedge (394*) (L A White) ...	W M Perrin	4 12 0	86	-	-
00-	Sayaist (Mrs M White)	K A Ryan	4 11 12	-	-	-
6080-52	Oceanist (USA) (369F) (Bill Preece)	B Preece	5 11 11	82	-	-
16P-242	Prix Du Nord (USA) (403F) (R A Jeffries)	K G Wingrove	4 11 4	75	-	-
24101/0-	Stone Madness (D2)—cso 2¾m h - (J Stone)	A R Davison	6 11 2	73	-	-
056-6	Sexton Boy (402*) (C C Trietline)	C C Trietline	5 10 10	67	-	-
6P-P	Light Dancer (368) (L J Codd)	L J Codd	4 10 4	61	-	-

Favourites: 3 1 1 0 1 2 0 0 2 2 Age: 6 5 4 6 8 5 6 6 5 6

1. STONE MADNESS 2. Oceanist 3. Rowhedge

2.45 Coventry Cable Television Novices' Chase 2¾m

£3150 added to stakes for 5-y-o and up which, at the start of the current season, have not won a chase £25 to enter Wts: 5-y-o 10st 10lb; 6-y-o and up 11st Mares allwd 5lb Pen, a winner of a chase 6lb Of 2 chases 10lb a surcharge will be levied on this race Closed on Sept 3

Form	Horse (Owner)	Trainer	Age-Wt	OR	SW	
0-S1211	Pinemartin (340*) (Mrs A G Martin)	G W Richards	7 11 10	92	-	-
P-321P2	Famous Run (347²) (Mrs J M Curson)	B Richmond	10 11 6	75	-	-
02231-1	Sibton Abbey (347*) (G A Hubbard)	F Murphy	5 11 2	-	-	-
4PP2PP-	Mr Kirby (J F O'Donovan)	A P Jones	8 11 0	-	-	-
000FP-4	New Outlook (395⁴) (Mrs J K Marshall)	G B Balding	6 11 0	80	-	-

0060/3-P	Phillipstown Lad (397) (F K Baxter)	T W Donnelly	7 11 0	-	-	-
004/350-	Prince Klenk (D) (J Stone)	A R Davison	9 11 0	-	-	-
33332-4	Sailor's Delight (150^4) –bl ch– (T P M McDonagh Ltd)	W A Stephenson	6 11 0	89	-	-
0-1332F	Singing Flame (406) (Garry Roberts)	J G M O'Shea	8 11 0	80	-	-
510P1-4	Sky Venture (224^4) (W Ebury) ...	C C Tristine	6 11 0	-	-	-
41/564-1	Thurlestone (NZ) (395*) (Ron Miller)	Capt T A Forster	7 11 0	92	-	-
02F3F-2	Upham Rainbow (177^2) –bl h– (R E Brinkworth)	D R Gandolfo	7 11 0	-	-	-
12/24-22	Wayward Singer (D) (323^2)–cse 2¾m h - bl ch, odds on– (John R Upson)	J R Upson	7 11 0	-	-	-
10P0/60/	William Anthony (D2) (Insight Cartons Ltd)	M C Pipe	8 11 0	-	-	-
-13	Winters Hill (367^3) (G B Balding)	G B Balding	6 11 0	-	-	-
0/0-	Anstey Boy (Shadowfax Racing) ...	C N Allen	5 10 10	-	-	-
2-4	Strong Approach (327^4) –bl ch– (W A Stephenson)	W A Stephenson	5 10 10	-	-	-

Favourites: 0 0 2 2 1 1 2 2 3 1   Age: 8 6 6 7 9 6 7 6 7 8

1. [illegible] 2. Thurlestone 3. [illegible] Abbey

3.15 Bbc Cwr Handicap Chase 2m

£3500 added to stakes for 5-y-o and up-Rated 0-125 £30 to enter Pen, after Sept 1st, a winner of a chase 7lb BBC COVENTRY AND WARWICK RADIO have very kindly contributed towards the prize money for this race Closed on Sept 3 TOPWEIGHT OFFICIALLY RATED 128

				OR		SW
111-111	Full Strength (D6) (399*) (J N G Moreton)	G Richards	7 12 3	128	46h	46h
211111-	Thar-An-Sharr (D7)–cse 2m ch - (John R Upson)	J R Upson	8 11 13	124	47g	-
602521-	Broad Beam (D12)–cse 2m ch (2) - (George James Webb)	P J Hobbs	10 11 4	115	51f	-
312-223	Kamaizak (D4) (274^3)–cse 2m h, 2½m ch - bl hcp ch– (Mrs P Joynes)	K S Bridgwater	9 10 12	109	46h	-
2113-11	Nearly Ready (D3) (349*) (John R Upson)	John R Upson	7 10 12	108	42g	-
440-222	Riva's Touch (USA) (D2) (312^2) (Mrs A L M King)	Mrs A L M King	7 10 2	99	-	-
51112-3	Court Rapier (D4) (369^3) (H V Perry)	Mrs H Parrott	8 10 6	97	42g	-
F63U-14	Master Vince (D8) (315^4)–cse 2m h, 2m ch - (Stanley Squires)	J White	12 10 0	97	50s	-
222213-	Le Bambino (Miss Julie Barrow)	R Barrow	13 8 11	80	-	-
213F4/P-	Nonstop (D3) (H Harpur-Crewe)	T W Donnelly	11 8 11	80	-	-
P/0P0/F1	Popthorn (358*) (Ian M McCready)	J P D Elliott	7 8 11	80	-	-

Favourites: 0 2 0 0 1 0 0 1 2 2   Age: 10 7 7 6 8 8 8 7 6 6

1. FULL STRENGTH (nap) 2. Thar-An-Sharr 3. Nearly Ready

3.45 Blundell Group Novices' Claiming Hurdle 2m

£2000 added to stakes for 4-y-o and up which, at the start of the current season, have not won a hurdle, each claimable at or above their specified price £20 to enter Wts: 4-y-o 11st 9lb; 5-y-o and up 11st 12lb Fillies and mares allwd 5lb Allowances: For each £500 below the maximum published price of £14000 1lb (Minimum published price £5000) THE BLUNDELL GROUP, of Coventry, have very kindly contributed towards the prize money for this race, including a trophy value £100, at the option of the winner If an allowance of weight is being claimed in respect of the claiming price, the claiming price and weight MUST be stated Only one such claiming price can be accepted Closed on Sept 3

				OR		SW
000/533-	Starchy Blake (L Munro)	R R Lamb	5 11 12	-	-	-
P0-	Jomana (M M Nashar)	J C Fox	4 11 4	-	-	-
0-	Kiwi Taska (NZ) (Mrs Julia Ward)	M H B Robinson	7 11 4	-	-	-
50-	Knowsleace (Mrs M R Q Henriques)	M Henriques	4 11 4	-	-	-
0000/	Westmead (A J K Dunn)	A J K Dunn	5 11 4	-	-	-
0B000-5	Damaneur (USA) (398^3) (Dr Kenneth S Fraser)	G Richards	4 11 1	85	-	-
0-	Electric Dancer (H Lodge)	C A Horgan	4 11 1	-	-	-
22334-	Athens Gate (USA) –bl h– (G A S Nicholls)	K A Ryan	6 11 0	-	39g	-
5/30/30-	Quiet Riot (Mrs J V Wilkinson)	J White	8 11 0	80	-	-
0P04P-	Rosemichael (Mrs Philippa L C Wyer)	G A Ham	6 11 0	-	-	-

43/5PP-	Tropico (Joneve)	I P Wardle	7	11	0	-	-	-
503233-	Ullswater (A G Thomas)	F Jordan	4	10	13	91	-	-
-4	Ghilan (USA) (398⁴) (Micky Burt) ..	R Akehurst	4	10	11	-	-	-
R/2U2	Royal Hunt (368²) (M Braycotton)	W Clay	5	10	11	-	-	-
080-	Fearsome (Unicorn Bloodstock And Racing Ltd)	K O Cunningham-Brown	4	10	10	72	-	-
00P0-31	Mister Tuftie (415*) (Major I C Straker)	G Richards	5	10	10	-	-	-
34PF30-	Legal Tina (S A Walker)	S Dow	5	10	9	91	-	-
/00/0-5	Balanced Realm (USA) (384⁶) (Dee Mechanical Services Limited)	T Casey	7	10	8	59	-	-
UU/35-12	Bonnie Boy (311²) (A P Moore)	R G Frost	10	10	8	82	-	-
4265-21	Bright Sapphire (D) (384*) (N Pay) .	D Burchell	4	10	8	83	-	-
0/5032-	Emerald Sunset (C Batt)	A R Davison	5	10	8	73	-	-
	Fast And Free (Mrs V L Walker) ..	P J Feilden	4	10	7	-	-	-
03-32F1	Spar Lady (D) (374*) (A G Mogford)	J D Roberts	7	10	7	76	-	-
	Adeline Lynn (Dale (Bloodstock) Ltd)	N Tinkler	4	10	6	-	-	-
	Ever Reckless (B P Monkhouse) ...	D T Thom	4	10	6	-	-	-
	Milclere (J Rose)	J A Glover	4	10	6	-	-	-
PPP/	Darlin' Again (Mrs S Armytage)	Mrs S Armytage	6	10	5	-	-	-
-0	Flight Again (398⁹) (Miss J Bunn)	K G Wingrove	4	10	5	-	-	-
00-F	Porridge Oats (264) (R C F Faiers)	R J Eckley	5	10	5	-	-	-
-3	Rusolble Cat (USA) (273²) (R G Levin)	B J McMath	4	10	5	-	-	-
0/55P-F4	Tudor D'Or (324⁴) —bf hcp h- (Mrs S M Somers)	R Lee	7	10	5	87	-	-
0-	Priory Bay (J C Fox)	J C Fox	4	10	4	-	-	-
2U554-6	Annie McGrath (405⁴) (Mrs J A Skelton)	R Lee	7	10	3	-	-	-
P/	Pecking Order (F J Yardley)	F J Yardley	6	10	3	-	-	-
0FP-	Spring Wedding (John Webber)	J Webber	5	10	3	-	-	-
354-244	Maple Hayes (384⁴) (Vivian Guy)	Mrs A Knight	4	10	0	59	-	-
00P-	Woodlands Lady (John Poiston)	Miss S J Wilton	4	10	0	-	-	-
435021-	Daily Sport Soon (D2)—cse 2m h - $(John Livock)	J R Jenkins	5	n	q	110	53g	-
0/0500-3	Dick Knight (346³) (Miss T J Bond)	J R Jenkins	9	n	q	89	-	-

Favourites: 1 2 0 0 3 0 1 0 0 3   Age: 4 4 8 5 4 6 5 4 6 4

1. [illegible] 2. Quiet Riot 3. Tropico

4.15 City Of Coventry Trophy Handicap Chase 2¾m

£3700 added to stakes for 5-y-o and up-Rated 0-136 £30 to enter Pen, after Sept 1st, a winner of a chase 6lb THE CITY OF COVENTRY have kindly presented the trophy value £200, at the option of the winner, included in the value of this race Closed on Sept 3
TOPWEIGHT OFFICIALLY RATED 132

						OR		SW
242P-32	Welsh Oak (D) (355²)—cse 2m h, 2¾m h - (G E Amey)	D R Gandolfo	10	12	0	132	55g	28f
-111-111	Full Strength (398*) (J N G Moreton)	G Richards	7	11	10	128	53h	53h
22P140-	Gembridge Jupiter (D5)—cse 2¾m h, 2¾m ch (2) - (Anthony Carver)	C C Trietline	12	11	7	125	36f	-
F1P4-21	Tartan Trademark (365*) (The Edinburgh Woollen Mill Ltd)	G W Richards	8	11	6	124	44y	-
42103-1	John O'Dee (348*) (G A Hubbard) ..	F Murphy	7	11	1	119	-	-
P/23440-	Bad Trade (P Piller)	W A Stephenson	8	10	11	115	-	-
P/1/00P2-	Deep Impression (D) (N G Mills)	M Bradstock	11	10	10	114	-	-
1221-UP	Mister Feathers (399) (Mrs M Forde)	J S King	9	10	7	111	52g	-
312-223	Karnatak (D) (274²)—cse 2m h, 2¾m ch - bf hcp ch- (Mrs P Joynes)	K S Bridgwater	9	10	5	109	53h	-
231241-	Folk Dance (D)—cse 2¾m h - (British Thoroughbred R & B Plc)	G B Balding	8	10	5	109	-	-
31113-2	Erostin Floats (365²) (Mrs Diane Upson)	J R Upson	6	10	1	105	-	-
U1FP-21	Watermeet Down (312*) (R M E Wright)	P J Hobbs	7	9	8	98	-	-
0U123F-	Clear Call (FR) (D Jones)	J A C Edwards	5	9	1	91	-	-

Form	Horse (Owner)	Trainer	Age	Wt	OR		
4S4123-	Beech Park -bl ch, edds on- (J B R Morris)	D Nicholson	6	8 10	86	-	-
1/213-34	Foot Stick (322[4]) (Mrs T Pritchard)	Dr P L J Pritchard	14	8 7	83	-	-
5332P-5	Wise Cracker (338[5]) (Martin Webster)	B Richmond	9	8 6	82	-	-

Favourites: 0 1 0 1 1 2 1 1 1 1 Age: 11 10 9 10 11 9 10 11 7 9

1. WATERSMEET DOWN 2. Tartan Trademark 3. Erestin Feats

4.45 Lady Godiva Juvenile Novices' Hurdle 2m

£2000 added to stakes for 3-y-o only which, at the start of the current season, have not won a hurdle £20 to enter Wts: 10st 10lb each Fillies alwd 5lb Pen, for each hurdle won 6lb This race will not divide at entry, unless receiving in excess of 4 times the safety factor a surcharge will be levied on this race Closed on Sept 3

Form	Horse (Owner)	Trainer	Wt	OR	SW	
-U1	Phil-Blake (D) (350[1]) (K W C Readings)	C A Horgan	11 2	-	-	-
-1	Runway Romance (FR) (D) (158[1]) (Johnny Kendall)	P J Hobbs	11 2	-	-	-
-1	Safety (USA) (319[1]) (Keith Sturgis)	J White	11 2	-	-	-
-12	Babarooms Paradise (NZ) (D2) (236[2]) -bl h- (T H Ounsley)	J R Jenkins	10 11	-	-	-
-10	Swingtime Belle (D) (352[7]) (L V Wadge)	M P Muggeridge	10 11	-	-	-
-2	Alicante (326[2]) (R W Sansom)	P A Blockley	10 10	-	-	-
	Barchem (Mrs A P B Allen)	G A Pritchard-Gordon	10 10	-	-	-
	Bell Turret (M Shaw)	I Campbell	10 10	-	-	-
	Chiefs Kraal (NZ) (A Manning)	J R Jenkins	10 10	-	-	-
-3	Crazy River (213[3]) (Peter Bonner)	Mrs J Pitman	10 10	-	-	-
	Dynamic Quest (John A Taylor)	J A Bennett	10 10	-	-	-
-3	Dast (USA) (350[3]) (R A Jeffries)	K G Wingrove	10 10	-	-	-
	Ela-Yemou (Winning Post Racing Ltd)	C N Allen	10 10	-	-	-
-6	Elwadi (352[6]) (Orchid Racing & Bloodstock Limited)	M D I Usher	10 10	-	-	-
	Gift Premium (Mrs Julia Ward)	M H B Robinson	10 10	-	-	-
	Grey Tudor (Mrs Eileen Homewood)	C N Allen	10 10	-	-	-
	Henri Le Comte (Mrs J E M Powell)	M McCormack	10 10	-	-	-
	Kalaloo (A Saleh)	F Durr	10 10	-	-	-
	Khios (USA) (Miss E R Cameron)	F Durr	10 10	-	-	-
	Knight Of Kirkton (Mrs D Hammerson)	P J Jones	10 10	-	-	-
	Lyneeys Lad (R F Nutland)	J S King	10 10	-	-	-
	Quick Tempo (T Dyer)	C Weedon	10 10	-	-	-
-32	Sandsumo (298[2]) (H R Hewitt)	M H Tompkins	10 10	-	-	-
-F	Sir Nick (209) -bl h- (G S B Cooke)	N A Callaghan	10 10	-	-	-
	Sureas (R D Starke)	G A Ham	10 10	-	-	-
	Wave Master (A W Anderson)	G A Pritchard-Gordon	10 10	-	-	-
	Astrid Gilberto (Melvyn A Kneller)	B Richmond	10 5	-	-	-
-3023	Cadford Ballerina (326[3]) (Mrs P Joynes)	K S Bridgwater	10 5	-	-	-
	Falland (James Neville)	R J Holder	10 5	-	-	-
	First Exhibition (Vivian Guy)	Mrs A Knight	10 5	-	-	-
	Gisbelonde Girl (R A Bennett)	R A Bennett	10 5	-	-	-
	Grondola (Park Industrial Supplies (Wales) Ltd)	D Burchell	10 5	-	-	-
	Hardiheroine (Mrs E A Yearley)	M C Pipe	10 5	-	-	-
	Maple Walk (K H Fischer)	M E D Francis	10 5	-	-	-
	Melcombe (Mrs Margie Fearn)	M McCormack	10 5	-	-	-
	Pine Ridge Lady (John S Cunliffe)	S Dow	10 5	-	-	-
	Sagacious Lady (USA) (Anthony Andrews)	M R Channon	10 5	-	-	-
	Sarah Carter (D J Buckley)	A P James	10 5	-	-	-
	Tina's Angel (F Deely)	J C Fox	10 5	-	-	-
-22	Wolver Gold (352[2]) (A L Roberts)	J D Roberts	10 5	-	-	-

Favourites: - - - - - - 1 2 2 1 2

1. HARDIHEROINE 2. Barchem 3. Safety

5.15 Garrick Jubilee Challenge Cup, A Handicap Hurdle 2m
£2500 added to stakes for 4-y-o and up-Rated 0-125 £25 to enter Pen. after Sept 1st. a winner of a hurdle 7lb The Cup to be held by the winning owner until Aug 1st, 1991 Closed on Sept 3 TOPWEIGHT OFFICIALLY RATED 116

Form	Horse (Owner)	Trainer	Age	Wt	OR		SW
00413-1	**Frendly Fellow** (D8) (269*) (C D Norton)	F Jordan	6	12 0	116	30h	-
35021-	**Daily Sport Soon** (D2)—cse 2m h - (John Livock)	J R Jenkins	5	11 8	110	38g	-
111134-	**Festoum** (D4) —bf hcp h- (D M Stone)	R Akehurst	7	11 6	108	46g	-
1116-31	**Valtaki** (D6) (313*)—cse 2m h - (J R Salter)	L J Codd	5	11 6	108	34h	-
6215-31	**Palm House** (D3) (369*) (R Tyrer)	G W Richards	5	11 6	108	46f	33f
2153-21	**Hiram B Birdbath** (D2) (366*) (Gilt-Edged Thoroughbred Racing Plc)	J A Glover	4	11 1	103	-	-
F35351-	**Bickerman** (D5) (B Dowling)	J L Spearing	7	10 12	100	-	-
1022-F2	**Island Jetsetter** (D) (317^{2}) (Robinson Publications Limited)	N Tinkler	4	10 12	100	-	-
031163-	**Murphy** (D4) —bf hcp h- (J P J Coles)	S E Sherwood	6	10 11	99	42g	-
10/004/0	**Knocksennie** (D2) (269*) (Brian J D Lewis)	R Lee	7	10 7	95	-	-
21530-	**Easy Over (USA)** (D) (Miss V Foster)	G M Moore	4	10 7	95	-	-
311-464	**Pressure Game** (D6) (366*) (Minizen Ltd)	K R Burke	7	10 6	94	-	-
240533-	**Squadron (CAN)** (D) (Pipe Scudamore Racing Plc)	M C Pipe	7	10 4	92	-	-
34PF30-	**Legal Tiss** (S A Walker)	S Dow	5	10 3	91	-	-
431-	**Billsha** (D)—cse 2m h - (A S Blackham)	B R Cambidge	4	10 3	91	-	-
416532-	**Tribal Mascot (USA)** (W H Dore)	D R Gandolfo	5	10 2	90	-	-
6P05/32-	**St Louis Blues** (H D White)	J A C Edwards	5	9 12	86	-	-
430-345	**Fingers Crossed** (D4) (416*) (G A S Nicholls)	K A Ryan	6	9 6	80	-	-
06005/F-	**El Capistrano** (D)—cse 2m h - (B Llewellyn)	B Llewellyn	9	9 5	79	-	-
6P-P	**Light Dancer** (368) (L J Codd)	L J Codd	4	8 1	61	-	-

Favourites: 1 0 1 0 0 0 1 2 3 1 Age: 5 4 4 5 6 6 4 6 6 8 5

1. VALTAKI 2. Frendly Fellow 3. Palm House

STRATEGY 6:

Trainers' Long-distance Raiders

As we have just seen, extensive journeys to racecourses can provide the horse racing enthusiast with profitable pointers, which is why some daily newspapers try to supply information on travelling racehorses as sophisticated as that in the *Racing Post* or the *Sporting Life*. Interestingly, in August 1995 these newspapers revealed that one particular racehorse was making a marathon journey to a racetrack. In fact, Carmentia's round trip of 720 miles from Newmarket to Ayr paid off handsomely for his trainer Sir Mark Prescott, since this two-year-old 'brought home the bacon' at 9–4. This was a pleasant reward for those of us who were sufficiently astute and energetic to do our geography homework, and who had noted that Prescott often sends runners on successful long-distance raids.

I therefore recommend that if you see that the 'leading trainers' table' for a particular racecourse contains the name of a handler who hails far from it, it is worth scrutinising any runners he has sent there. Unfortunately, the *Daily Express* has abandoned its former practice of placing a large 'T' by the names of horses travelling long distances to race meetings. If you wish to capitalise on the belief that horses, especially those from small yards, are unlikely to undertake marathon journeys to racecourses for nothing, you will need to check the *Racing Post*, or a good map and Raceform's *Horses in Training*.

Incidentally, it was Lord George Bentinck who first alerted the racegoing public to the claims of long-distance 'raiders'. This prominent Victorian owner was aware that, in 1816, a horse had been transported from Worcester in a padded bullock cart to race at Newmarket and so hit upon the ingenious idea of running Elis (his 1835 Molecomb Stakes winner) so frequently in the South during the summer, that few would feel he was likely to line up for the Doncaster St. Leger early in September. Indeed, Bentinck took pains to publicise the presence of Elis in his Goodwood stable ten days prior to the Classic so that serious doubt over whether the colt would be asked to complete an exhausting walk all the way from Goodwood to Doncaster would cause his price to lengthen in the ante-post betting market. The ruse worked and Bentinck's commission agent was able to secure attractive odds against Elis before Lord George spirited him up North in a 'horse van' drawn by four horses!

Obviously, mounting a long-distance raid often calls for elaborate precautions to ensure that nothing goes amiss with the raider in transit. Sometimes, however, the racecourses where horses finally arrive are so topographically dissimilar to the scenes of their past triumphs, or the weather and atmospheric conditions on these tracks so different from those these horses have left at home, that the best laid plans of their ambitious connections 'gang awry'. This was surely the case with Dancing Brave at Santa Anita in 1986 and as it happens, I recently came across some comments made 33 years ago about the performance of English racehorses on the Californian track, by Terence Downing. If Guy Harwood had read these words he may have thought twice about sending Dancing Brave to run there. Writing in the March, 1954 edition of the *Racing Review,* Downing commented that when he first went racing at Santa Anita and took stock of the horses which were snapping up highly considered trifles of the American turf, it struck him that for some of the better English horses these would prove 'money for old rope'. Then he noticed something. There were at that time nine or ten imported horses which he had seen running in Britain, but not one of them was running within 2st of its British form. The answer, Downing finally decided, lay in this business of acclimatising. Downing suggested that British horses running at Santa Anita would put up lacklustre performances (such as Dancing Brave's fifth to Manila) due to changes in their blood density caused by their transferring from a cool climate to the heat haze of California. Downing's theory was that the blood of British horses suffering from what one might term 'climate lag' was 25% over proof, which meant that a good deal of strain was imposed on their hearts if they were asked to race before it had been given time to thin out!

I am not, of course, suggesting that horses sent from Scottish stables to race straightaway at Brighton are likely to disappoint for the climatic reasons that might explain the failure of Dancing Brave! What may possibly help or hinder a long-distance raider, however, is whether the racecourse it runs at is to be found at a lower or a higher altitude than the training grounds on which it performs. Incidentally, readers wishing to research the whole question of whether 'altitudinal' factors influence racing performance are advised to purchase Ordnance Survey Maps or past copies of the *Sun* newspaper whose racing page used to reveal the heights above sea level at which British tracks have been constructed!

STRATEGY 7:

Doubles and Trebles Specialists

The so-called Gay Future affair, so dramatic, controversial and colourful that it brought hilarity to courtrooms and provided a first rate storyline for one of the best racing programmes ever shown on television, represented an ingenious way of landing a coup on a single horse that looked as if it featured, along with two other horses, in a treble. These, of course, were always intended to be non-runners and did not ever leave their boxes in Scotland to run at lowly Cartmel!

Some racehorse trainers are such brilliant legitimate tacticians that they actually succeed in planning and bringing off what the perpetrators of the Gay Future affair never intended – more than one win on the same racing day. One such trainer was J. P. Hudson, who trained in a fairly modest, but extremely shrewd, way at Lambourn. As it happened, I knew of this trainer's spectacular feat in once pulling off a massive long odds accumulator. The horses concerned were Careful Lad at 8–11, Radish and Lemon at 3–1 and the well-named Absolutely Perfect, at 11–2. Hudson and an army of punters who placed small doubles, trebles and four-timers in many London and Hertfordshire betting shops would have pulled off the biggest (legitimate) coup since the Gay Future affair had a fourth Hudson-trained runner managed to prevail! So, I took due note when, earlier this decade, I saw that Hudson had booked top jockeys, Ray Cochrane and Willie Carson, for 'outside' rides on his runners in two successive races. The first survived a photograph and a stewards' enquiry to win at 33–1 and the second, after being 'nibbled at' at 10–1 after opening at 7–1, triumphed at 9–1 by the large margin of 1½ lengths to give Hudson a 297–1 double!

It will certainly pay you to look for small trainers like P. Nicholls and owners too such as R. Ogden, who occasionally seek to make one particular racing day a spectacularly profitable one. Since no publication records the multiple daily wins of trainers, you will need to keep your own records of these and use hindsight to discover (as with Cochrane's and Carson's bookings) whether any particular arrangements augur well. One word of warning though – it will pay to ignore the many multiple daily successes achieved by large yards that cast their nets far and wide and 'overbait the river'. What you need to note from *Horses in Training* are yards with few inmates in them that manage to get more than one of their charges into the winners' enclosure on the same racing day. I recommend that you concentrate on handlers responsible for less than thirty horses who achieve this feat since they may well return to the same racing 'well' to take yet another deep and long sustaining drink!

STRATEGY 8:

Trainers in Form

One of the reasons, of course, why many trainers manage to win more than one race on one racing day, or over several successive ones, is because very often a stable's winners tend to come in batches or 'waves'. The trick, of course, is to be able to spot such a 'form wave' whilst it has some way to run and not just before it is about to break! Indeed, if like a surfer you can take advantage of the 'mileage' such a wave can offer, you can enjoy an exhilarating experience as it carries you into quite spectacular profit.

As it happens, some seasons ago I read a particularly interesting contribution to a systems column of a racing periodical that was sent in by a correspondent known as Old Charlie. His approach was to list alphabetically what he rather vaguely called the 'top twenty' trainers in a lined exercise book. The backer was then instructed to take the previous day's results and allot points for any placings their runners had achieved – four for a winner, three for a second, two for a third (in one of 12 or more runners). Old Charlie further recommended that, after this procedure had been adopted eleven times, the first column of points be crossed through and disregarded so that your daily assessment of stables in form would thus involve the past ten racing days.

Old Charlie's point is that tabular indications of when leading yards are coming into, or going out of, form is highly revealing. No doubt, he was delighted to see the recent introduction of a new guide to winner finding in the form of a daily feature of the *Sporting Life's* form coverage. This, aptly styled as 'Trainerform', has justifiably been described as consisting of the 'most comprehensive charts ever devised to provide a day-to-day guide to the current form of trainers (and, incidentally, of jockeys). In fact, these Trainerform charts do much that would appeal to Old Charlie in that they provide a detailed breakdown of trainers' performances over the past 28 days. Most usefully too, they show how many runners a yard has had since it sent out a winner – a key factor in trying to determine which form waves to avoid because they may have run their course!

STRATEGY 9:

Owner-Trainers

The fact that 'Formaster', in my view one of the very best computer programmes for winner finding, credits runners with bonus points for being owner-trained is one very good reason why you should give such contenders more than a passing glance. Indeed, the few inches that prevented Musical Moments from prevailing in a Warwick seller once cost me a fortune after, foolishly, I failed to support this bay colt each way at 14–1 and then tantalisingly saw him beaten by a far shorter-priced runner that would probably not have won, had he carried his originally allocated weight. The reason why I plunged on Musical Moments was not just because he was top-rated on Formaster's computer print-out, but because he had been sent to race in the Midlands by his shrewd Taunton-based owner-trainer, J. D. Roberts.

Fortunately, my losses were recovered with the victories of many other successful owner-trained runners. Indeed, at the time of writing, trainer Clive Brittain's success at 10–1 with his own Sacred Mirror (which I supported for, like Musical Moments, figuring as an owner-trained runner in the first three in the betting forecast) has enlivened an otherwise lacklustre day at a Lingfield all weather meeting.

Recent research into a full season's record of successes for owner-trainers also reveals that handlers M. J. Fetherstone-Godley, C. Egerton, J. White, Bob Jones, R. Akehurst, S. Dow, Mrs. M. Reveley and Mrs. J. Ramsden often succeed with their own horses or those of syndicates carrying their names.

4.25 CENTURION FILLIES HANDICAP
(£3,089: 1m 4f) (7 runners)

601	(5)	2630-12	WILD STRAWBERRY 9 (C,BF,F,G) (Copyforce) Miss B Sanders 7-10-0	D Biggs	94
602	(3)	01400-6	ELLY FLEETFOOT 21 (G) (A Reid) B Meehan 4-8-12	G Hannon (7)	90
603	(4)	5/05055-	SACRED MIRROR 270 (C Brittain) C Brittain 5-8-11	M Larsen	90
604	(1)	550040-	UNCHARTED WATERS 109 (F) (R Cyzer) C Cyzer 5-8-8	J Fortune	95
605	(6)	0305-25	NEVER SO RITE 14 (F) (J Gutkin) D Arbuthnot 4-8-5	R Cochrane	99
606	(2)	221036-	ALL THE JOYS 92 (C,S) (Mrs G Gooderham) C Cyzer 5-8-3	J Quinn	94
607	(7)	204-465	SWYNFORD FLYER 7 (F,G) (D Pettifor) J A Harris 7-7-10	C Adamson (7)	96

BETTING: 9-4 Wild Strawberry, 7-2 Sacred Mirror, 6-1 Never So Rite, 8-1 All The Joys, Elly Fleetfoot, 10-1 others.

1995: CARPATHIAN 4-8-9 D Harrison (6-4 fav) Lord Huntingdon 8 ran

PART TWO: SIDING WITH JOCKEYS

STRATEGY 10:

Jockeys for Trainers

Since most jockeys are busy riding and travelling to race meetings, many employ agents to arrange their rides and I find it often pays to monitor their mounts most carefully. You should also keep in mind the fact that betting coups are often entrusted to the capable hands of so-called 'job-jockeys', who can be relied upon to 'bring home the bacon' when the money is down (as Sir Gordon Richards had so often to do in his early riding days). Fortunately the *Racing Post* provides detailed information on the performances of jockeys course by course which also indicates the trainers for whom they have proved most successful in recent seasons. Such data can help you to produce a necessarily select list of jockeys to follow.

Interestingly, my own scrutiny of the *Racing Post's* information on trainers and jockeys to note at Lingfield early in February 1996 indicated that, of the jockeys shown in this newspaper's exhaustively researched 'Top Jockeys' table for this all-weather flat racecourse, two had 'wins to runs' percentages, when riding for particular trainers, of 33 or more.

As can be seen from this particular table that appears on page 48, these jockeys were R. Cochrane and T. Ives. The problem, of course, was how to decide which of their seemingly very significant bookings – Cochrane's for Rakis for trainer M. Brittain and that of Ives for the Paul Smith trained Old Hook in the same 3.55 race – was the more portentous.

As it happened, this problem was easy to solve. This was because I made sure I followed a differentiation procedure whose value has been proved over many years. This involves, when a selection method throws up several qualifiers, giving one's preference to the shortest-priced qualifier.

As Rakis was the 2–1 forecast favourite (doubtless for having won his last three races) he seemed very likely to me to be able to get the measure of Old Hook whose 7–1 quote in the betting forecast perhaps reflected the fact that he had not raced for 70 days and was having his first run of the 1996 season. It was pleasing to see Rakis run out a worthy winner as the well-backed 11–8 favourite under job-jockey Cochrane.

LINGFIELD TOP JOCKEYS

Flat 1992+ *WITH RIDES TODAY*

WINS-RIDES			TRAINER *SUPPLYING RIDES TODAY* GIVING BEST COURSE RECORD	WINS-RIDES		ALL RIDES £1 STAKE	COURSE RIDES SINCE WIN
60-248	24%	**J Weaver**	*M Johnston*	**11**-37	30%	**+45.27**	0
46-258	18%	**R Cochrane**	*M Brittain*	**3**-6	50%	–26.75	0
41-409	10%	**D Biggs**	*R J O'Sullivan*	**21**-129	16%	–166.98	9
29-503	6%	**J Quinn**	*J J Bridger*	**2**-21	10%	–290.95	14
26-220	12%	**A Clark**	*Miss Gay Kelleway*	**0**-1	0%	–63.45	5
22-130	17%	**S Whitworth**	*G L Moore*	**7**-33	21%	–15.07	1
21-275	8%	**N Adams**	*M Johnston*	**2**-8	25%	–57.42	3
20-114	18%	**T Ives**	*Paul Smith*	**2**-3	67%	**+1.42**	2
19-125	15%	**G Duffield**	*Sir M Prescott*	**12**-39	31%	–37.61	0
17-191	9%	**S Sanders**	*A Moore*	**2**-8	25%	–67.50	12
12-93	13%	**P McCabe**	*P T Dalton*	**0**-2	0%	**+17.50**	8
7-45	16%	**Amanda Sanders**	*Mrs N Macauley*	**6**-29	21%	**+9.50**	2
7-70	10%	**M Wigham**	*R Hollinshead*	**1**-7	14%	–16.25	15
6-26	23%	**L Suthern**	*G L Moore*	**5**-18	28%	**+6.28**	3
6-38	16%	**J Fortune**	*P C Haslam*	**2**-18	11%	–7.00	2
6-85	7%	**M Fenton**	*R P C Hoad*	**0**-1	0%	–55.12	7
6-111	5%	**S Drowne**	*R J Hodges*	**2**-29	7%	–58.75	14

3.55 *Jervis Handicap (Class D)* SIS

Winner £3,566.25 **7f(AW)**

11 declared

£5,100 added **For** 4yo+ Rated 0-80 **Minimum Weight** 7-10 **Penalties** after January 28th, a winner 6lb **Entries** 17 pay £25 **Penalty Value 1st** £3,566.25 **2nd** £1,080 **3rd** £527.50 **4th** £251.25

501-111 RAKIS (IRE) 9 CD — 6 10-2
1 *b/br g Alzao–Bristle* — **R Cochrane** (82)
(11) **M Brittain** P G Shorrock

62240-5 ABTAAL 9 D — 6 9-12
2 *b h Green Desert–Stufida* — **S Drowne** (3) (65)
(7) **R J Hodges** P Slade

22F141- **OLD HOOK (IRE)** 70 CD — 5 9-11
3 *b/br h Digamist–Day Dress* — **T Ives** (81)
(4) **Paul Smith (BEL)** R Van Slemsbrouck

1021-77 DUKE VALENTINO 14 CD — 4 9-9
4 *br c Machiavellian–Aldhabyih* — **M Wigham** (82)
(10) **R Hollinshead** J E Bigg

20759-1 **SOAKING** 16 CD — 6 9-4
5 *b g Dowsing–Moaning Low* — **J Weaver** (78)
(8) **P Burgoyne** Philip Saunders

448-282 INVOCATION 7 CD — 9 9-2
6 *ch g Kris–Royal Saint* — **S Sanders** (79)
(6) **A Moore** Mr R Kiernan

09-5523 ULTRA BEET 7 CBF — v 4 9-2
7 *b g Puissance–Cassiar* — **J Fortune** (78)
(3) **P C Haslam** Pet Express Ltd T/A Nutrimix

7078**9-6 AGWA** 7 CD — 7 9-1
8 *b g Local Suitor–Meissarah* — **D Biggs** (73)
(2) **R J O'Sullivan** I A Baker

7018-44 TUIGAMALA 14 CD — 5 8-5
9 *b g Welsh Captain–Nelliellamay* — **N Adams** (81)
(9) **R Ingram** Roger Ingram

885000- **SCORPIUS** 129 — b 6 8-4
10 *b h Soviet Star–Sally Brown* — **J Stack** (3) (56)
(1) **T T Clement** Mrs C Clement

50**463-9 YO KIRI-B** 14 — 5 7-10
11 *b m Night Shift–Briar Creek* — **A Mackay** (77)
(5) **J Ffitch-Heyes** Miss L A Elliott

LONG HANDICAP: Yo Kiri-B **7-5**

1995 (7 ran) **Digpast** (4) R J O'Sullivan 5 8-6 OR52 — D Biggs 11/4C

BETTING FORECAST: 2 Rakis, 9-2 Soaking, 5 Duke Valentino, 7 Old Hook, 8 Invocation, Ultra Beet, 10 Tuigamala, 14 Agwa, 16 Abtaal, 25 Scorpius, Yo Kiri-B.

Interestingly, on the very same day as, at Lingfield, Rakis vindicated the wisdom of siding with especially booked jockeys, this particular strategy also achieved some interesting results at Sandown's jumping meeting. This time the *Racing Post's* 'Top Trainers' table for this course showed that three jockeys had, when riding for particular stables, wins to runs ratios of one in three or better. These, as can be seen from the table below, were G. McCourt, when riding for R. Hannon, C. Llewellyn, when teaming up with J. Old, and J. F. Titley when riding runners sent to race at Sandown by Henrietta Knight.

SANDOWN TOP JOCKEYS

Jumps 1991/92+ *WITH RIDES TODAY*

WINS-RIDES			TRAINER *SUPPLYING RIDES TODAY* GIVING BEST COURSE RECORD	WINS-RIDES		ALL RIDES £1 STAKE	COURSE RIDES SINCE WIN
33-113	29%	**R Dunwoody**	*S Dow*	**2**-2	100	**+19.49**	2
20-98	20%	**A Maguire**	*D Nicholson*	**8**-25	32%	–9.66	1
16-109	15%	**J Osborne**	*O Sherwood*	**6**-37	16%	–52.29	6
9-53	17%	**P Hide**	*J T Gifford*	**9**-49	18%	**+2.20**	3
7-34	21%	**G McCourt**	*R Hannon*	**1**-3	33%	–11.21	0
7-59	12%	**G Bradley**	*C P E Brooks*	**4**-24	17%	–7.12	4
6-32	19%	**A P McCoy**	*J T Gifford*	**1**-1	100	–4.62	0
5-23	22%	**W Marston**	*Mrs J Pitman*	**2**-10	20%	**+7.60**	5
5-41	12%	**C Llewellyn**	*J A B Old*	**2**-4	50%	**+28.50**	23
4-30	13%	**D Bridgwater**	*M C Pipe*	**0**-1	0%	–5.64	5
3-13	23%	**J Titley**	*Miss H C Knight*	**1**-3	33%	–0.75	3
3-19	16%	**C Maude**	*N A Twiston-Davies*	**0**-9	0%	–2.25	7
3-23	13%	**P Niven**	*Mrs M Reveley*	**2**-15	13%	–8.62	7
3-25	12%	**S McNeill**		**0**-0	0%	–13.75	5

McCourt was due to ride the shortest-priced Sandown qualifier that had the edge over Llewellyn's mount in the same race but, when this initial selection was withdrawn, my course became clear – an interest in Debutante Days, Jason Titley's significant looking mount on Henrietta Knight's appropriately named first-time-out 13–2 winner of Sandown's first race!

1.20 *Ripley Four Year Old Novices' Hurdle (Class C)* SIS

16 declared *Winner £6,935* (2m 110y) **2m½f**

£10,000 added **For** 4yo which, prior to May 1st, 1995, have not won a hurdle **Weights** 11st each **Penalties** a winner of a hurdle 4lb; of 2 hurdles, or of one value £3500 8lb **Allowances** fillies 5lb; horses which have not run in a hurdle 4lb **Entries** 35 pay £20 **Penalty Value 1st** £6,935 **2nd** £2,120 **3rd** £1,050 **4th** £515

No.	Form / Horse / Breeding / Trainer / Owner	Age & Weight / Jockey	Rating	Silks
1	531P222 **OCEAN HAWK (USA)** 15 D *b g Hawkster–Society Sunrise* **N A Twiston-Davies** Miss Jean Broadhurst	4 11-8 **C Llewellyn**	131	
2	112 **PADDY'S RETURN (IRE)** 49 DBF *b g Kahyasi–Bayazida* **F Murphy** P O'Donnell	4 11-8 **R Dunwoody**	124	
3	1118 **REVEILLON (GER)** 74 (13F) D *b c Keen–Ringawoody* **C Von Der Recke (GER)** B Raber	4 11-8 **K Hviid**		
4	1 **MISTINGUETT (IRE)** 21 D *b f Doyoun–Sidama* **N A Twiston-Davies** John Duggan	4 11-3 **T Jenks**	105	
5	3 **CLAIRESWAN (IRE)** 72 *ch g Rhoman Rule–Choclate Baby* **M H Tompkins** Claire and Beryl	4 11-0 **D Gallagher**	106	
6	P **INDONESIAN (IRE)** 28 *b/br g Alzao–Miss Garuda* **C P E Brooks** Uplands Bloodstock	b 4 11-0 **G Bradley**		
7	0 **MR CHRISTIE** 21 *b g Doulab–Hi There* **Miss L C Siddall** David Mann Partnership	4 11-0 **M Richards**	72	
8	8 **NAUTICAL JEWEL** 15 *b g Handsome Sailor–Kopjes* **M D I Usher** Sporting Partners	4 11-0 **G McCourt**		
9	3 **REAGANESQUE (USA)** 28 *b g Nijinsky–Basoof* **P G Murphy** Mrs John Spielman	4 11-0 **P Hide**	117	
10	P3 **SAILEP (FR)** 17 *ch c Holst–Sweet Cashmere* **R J Hodges** P Slade	4 11-0 **W McFarland**	106	
11	5 **TILAAL (USA)** 21 *ch c Gulch–Eye Drop* **M Hammond** Megan Dennis-Craig Shields	4 11-0 **P Niven**	91	
12	1P **GREENWAY LADY** 66 D *ch f Prince Daniel–Lady Ector* **Miss A Embiricos** Bradnock Syndicate	4 10-13 **J Ryan**	87	

13 **BIG TREAT** (IRE) (143F) — 4 10-10
b g Be My Guest–Cavurina — **D Bridgwater**
P W Hiatt P W Hiatt

14 **CULTURAL ICON** (USA) (16F) — 4 10-10
b c Kris S–Sea Prospector — **J Osborne**
P Mitchell Mrs Patricia Mitchell

15 **TOMAL** (23F) — 4 10-10
b g King Among Kings–Jacinda — **M A Fitzgerald**
R Ingram The Toilly Partnership

16 **DEBUTANTE DAYS** (115F) — 4 10-5
ch f Dominion–Doogali — **J Titley**
Miss H C Knight Mrs Shirley Brasher

1995 (11 ran) **Amancio** G Harwood 4 11-0 PM108 M Perrett 9/2

BETTING FORECAST: 9-4 Paddy's Return, 5-2 Ocean Hawk, 5 Mistinguett, 8 Debutante Days, 10 Reaganesque, 12 Reveillon, 16 Claireswan, Sailep, 20 Indonesian, Tilaal, 33 bar.

STRATEGY 11:

Jockeys for Owners

Interestingly, those who go racing (or who are canny enough to study form for major races in racing dailies that includes coloured studies of the jockeys' colours), can in the case of races in which mega-rich owners like Sheikh Mohammed have several runners, determine which of these is sporting the first, second or even the third colours. For instance, in a recent running of the prestigious King George VI and Queen Elizabeth Diamond Stakes, it came as something of a surprise to see that Henry Cecil's Belmez was sporting the second colours of Britain's most supportive owner, despite the fact that of the Sheikh's three runners in this race, this colt was 'out with the washing' in the morning betting at 12–1. Thus, I felt an each-way interest in this runner, rather than wagers at the poor odds available about the favourite, In the Wings, and the third favourite, Old Vic, was a 'bargain' and so it proved when Michael Kinane brought home Belmez from Old Vic a few hours later.

3.20 **King George VI And Queen Elizabeth Diamond Stakes (Group I) 1½m**

£300000 added to stakes for 3-y-o and up £1575 to enter, £1800 ex unless forfeit dec by Jul 10 £1125 ex if entry confirmed; Wts: 3-y-o colts and geldings 8st 9lb; fillies 8st 6lb 4-y-o and up colts and geldings 9st 7lb; fillies 9st 4lb A piece of plate presented by Her Majesty is included in the value of this race DE BEERS CONSOLIDATED MINES LTD have generously given £167000 included in the value of this race DE BEERS CONSOLIDATED MINES LTD will give a contribution to the travel expenses of runners from outside Europe in special circumstances DE BEERS CONSOLIDATED MINES LTD will give a Diamond award to the winning owner value £8000, included in the value of this race and, in addition, a Diamond award will be given to the trainer of the winner and to the winning jockey THERE WILL BE A PARADE FOR THIS RACE, ft dec for 12.

Penalty value £284,715; 2nd £106,365.75, 3rd £50,932.88, 4th £22,011.37

1 110-413 **ASSATIS (USA)**(18) **(D4)** **BBC 1**
(b H Topsider (USA) - Secret Asset (USA)),
-cse 1½m (3) - (S Harada)
G Harwood **5 9 7 ....M Shibata 9**

5 1/10-211 **IN THE WINGS**(27) **(D2)**
(b C Sadler's Wells (USA) - High Hawk)
(Sheikh Mohammed)
A Fabre (Fr) **4 9 7 ....C Asmussen 2**

10 11111-3 **OLD VIC**(36) **(D3)**
(b C Sadler's Wells (USA) - Cockade)
-bf odds on- (Sheikh Mohammed)
H R A Cecil **4 9 7 ....S Cauthen 1**

11 226-221 **SAPIENCE**(18) **(D)**
(ch C Niniski (USA) - Claretta (USA))
(W H O'Gorman)
J G FitzGerald **4 9 7 ....Pat Eddery 5**

13 1-113 **BELMEZ (USA)**(27) **(D)**
(b C El Gran Senor (USA) - Grace Note (FR))
(Sheikh Mohammed)
H R A Cecil **3 8 9 ....M J Kinane 11**

Eleven runners

FORECAST: 2 In The Wings, 100-30 Cacoethes, 5 Old Vic, 11-2 Sapience, 10 Terimon, 12 Belmez, 16 Husyan, 20 Legal Case, 20 Assatis, 25 Charmer, 1000 Limeburn.

Last Year: NASHWAN (USA), 8-8, W Carson, 2-9 (Major W R Hern) 7 ran.

Those who knew that Henry Cecil runs a non-gambling operation and often wins with his stable's second string would, on this occasion, have 'cleaned up' at Ascot on Belmez, for, as Danny Hall reveals in *How To Win On The Horses,* when this top-class colt made his debut in a Newmarket maiden the previous season at 50–1, Cecil also saddled the unsuccessful 2–1 chance Satin Wood!

STRATEGY 12:

Jockeys for Courses

The fact that Steve Donoghue used to be urged on in the Derby with cries of 'Come on Steve' reflected the belief that in his day, on the big occasion at Epsom, he was the jockey who would best cope with this track's highly idiosyncratic topography. Indeed, so it certainly proved when, in eleven successive runnings of the Blue Riband between 1915 and 1925, Donoghue prevailed on no less than six occasions! Naturally, I would not recommend any 'blind' following of a jockey on a particular racecourse.

Rather, as with Strategy 1 (which dealt with trainers for courses) it is vital to ensure that one takes a betting interest only when the two important factors of past excellence and outstanding impending prospects converge in a way that seems especially propitious.

It has often been wisely said that not even the best jockey can win without the horse and that is why I only rely on jockeys with excellent past records at certain racecourses if they happen to be about to ride horses that a private handicapper rates as having the best claims.

Of all the daily newspapers that cover racing, *The Times* is outstanding in including the names of horses' owners for the main meeting and, crucially, for including private handicap ratings for many runners.

I rely heavily on these ratings and when deciding which jockeys to side with firstly look in *The Times* to see which horses have been given the top form rating of 99. If, and only if, any of these are due to be ridden by one or other of the six jockeys that this newspaper also most usefully identifies as having the best course wins to rides ratios, do I consider getting involved in any betting. This was the case recently at Newton Abbot. Indeed, a momentary glance down the runners there revealed that, of the six runners given his top rating of 99 by the form expert of *The Times*, only Sister Stephanie in the 3.00 and Teraq, in the 4.00, were due to be partnered by one or other of the Devon course's six top jockeys. These two runners thus looked worthy of an interest and duly repaid this quite handsomely in winning at 4–6 and at 5–1 under Richard Dunwoody and David Bridgwater respectively.

COURSE SPECIALISTS

NEWTON ABBOT: Trainers: J Old, 7 winners from 20 runners, 35.0%; R O'Sullivan, 9 from 26, 34.6%; D Nicholson, 5 from 16, 31.3%; M Pipe, 93 from 324, 28.7%; P Nicholls, 24 from 94, 25.5%; J Edwards, 7 from 29, 24.1%. **Jockeys:** T Grantham, 3 winners from 9 rides, 33.3%; R Dunwoody, 51 from 172, 29.7%; D Bridgwater, 20 from 78, 25.6%; G McCourt, 12 from 50, 24.0%; B Clifford, 9 from 42, 21.4%.

NEWTON ABBOT

1.30 TEIGNMOUTH MAIDEN HURDLE
(£2,369: 2m 1f) (16 runners)

1	6	AMBLESIDE 114 Mrs S Williams 5-11-10	A Tory	72
2	3	CRACKING PROSPECT 83 B Millman 5-11-10	D Salter (5)	99
3		GOLDEN NEWS P Rodford 5-11-10	S Burrough	--
4	4-0	HOLDIMCLOSE 42 R Frost 6-11-10	J Frost	94
5	00P-	KIRSTY'S PAL 285 D Bloomfield 7-11-10	R Darke	--
6	P	MONEGHETTI 46 M Pipe 5-11-10	Jamie Evans	--
7		THINAMI R Hodges 7-11-10	T Dascombe (5)	--
8		TUDOR TOWN K Bishop 8-11-10	L Harvey	--
9	4003	UNCLE BERT 34 Mrs M McCourt 6-11-10	G McCourt	91
10	/00-	DANCING BAREFOOT 333 M Bolton 7-11-5	P Hide	--
11	54	HONEY BUN 7 (B) M Pipe 5-11-5	D Bridgwater	96
12	130	MY OLD CHINA 11 (F) A Foster 7-11-5	C Llewellyn	--
13	5P-	VALLEY'S CHOICE 262 S Stevens 7-11-5	Mr L Jefford	--
14		GOLDEN POUND 5F Miss G Kelleway 4-10-12	R Dunwoody	--
15		MU-TADIL 124F R Baker 4-10-12	B Powell	--
16	40	UNITED FRONT 5 R O'Sullivan 4-10-12	D O'Sullivan	92

NEWTON ABBOT

3.00 (3m2f110y nov ch): **SISTER STEPHANIE** (R Dunwoody, 4-6F) 1; **Court Melody** (11-4) 2; **Beaurepaire** (9-1) 3. 5 ran. 8, dist. (Mrs M McCourt). Tote: win £1.30; places £1.10, £1.90. Dual F'cast: £1.90. CSF: £2.84.

4.00 (2m5f110y h'cap ch): **TERAO** (D Bridgwater, 5-1) 1; **Bramblehill Buck** (7-2JF) 2; **Pop Song** (15-2) 3. 8 ran. Super Tactics 7-2JF. 5, hd. (M Pipe). Tote: win £6.40; places £2.10, £2.00, £1.80. Dual F'cast: £6.00. CSF: £21.57. Tricast: £117.36. Trio: £98.30. NR: Maple Dancer.

2.00 HOECHST PANACUR EBF MARES NATIONAL HUNT NOVICES HURDLE (£2,549: 2m 6f) (16)

1	-461	MISS DISKIN 7 (D,S) R Buckler 7-11-5	B Powell	99
2	2-16	QUEENFORD BELLE 18 (G,S) Miss H Knight 6-11-5	G F Ryan (5)	90
3	-231	SILVER SHRED 16 (F,S) M Pipe 5-11-5	O Burrows (7)	88
4	50	CARMEL'S JOY 39 T George 7-10-12	R Dunwoody	--
5	40-0	CERIDWEN 33 T Greathead 6-10-12	W Humphreys	--
6	6-P0	CRAVATE 4 Mrs J Mills 6-10-12	D Salter (5)	--
7	600	DEARDS SMASHER 32 N Smith 7-10-12	J Ryan	--
8	10	LA BELLA VILLA 37 (F) N Twiston-Davies 6-10-12	C Llewellyn	--
9	0	LADY NOSO 11 Mrs J Pitman 5-10-12	R Farrant	80
10	00-	NOMINATION GOLD 296 B Palling 6-10-12	C Maude	--
11	6	POLLYDALUS 58 Mrs M McCourt 5-10-12	B Clifford	--
12	060	QUINAG 33 K Bailey 5-10-12	T J Murphy (3)	--
13		SEASONS Mrs D Thomas 7-10-12	A Larnach (3)	--
14	FP	THIRD MELODY 17 (F) J Mullins 10-10-12	S Curran (3)	--
15	0/0	UP THE TEMPO 52 P Farrell 7-10-12	J R Kavanagh	--
16	0P-0	VEXFORD MODEL 215 V Greenway 6-10-12	Guy Lewis (3)	63

9-4 Silver Shred, 3-1 Queenford Belle, 9-2 Miss Diskin, 7-1 La Bella Villa, 16-1 Lady Noso, 20-1 Quinag, 25-1 others.

2.30 NEWTON ABBOT SELLING HANDICAP CHASE (£2,857: 2m 110yd) (10)

1	0P6-	GOLDEN OPAL 266 (D,G,S) R Buckler 11-12-0	B Powell	--
2	0-2P	SOVEREIGN NICHE 4 (V,F,G,S) M Pipe 8-11-11	D Bridgwater	91
3	-5P4	AGRA 74 (B,CD,S) M Pipe 8-11-9	Jamie Evans	91
4	-302	EVENING RAIN 54 (CD,F,G,S) R Hodges 10-11-4	R Dunwoody	98
5	-653	PRUDENT PEGGY 56 (G,S) R Frost 9-11-1	J Frost	89
6	/F/	MARTIN'S FRIEND 751 (F,S) D Bloomfield 13-10-13	R Darke	--
7	25PU	EMRAL MISS 7 (B) C Popham 8-10-7	T Dascombe (5)	88
8	6542	FULL SHILLING 37 (V,BF) K Burke 7-10-1	A Larnach (3)	99
9	0-P0	DAVES DELIGHT 21 (S) Miss S Waterman 10-10-0	Mr G Shenkin (7)	--
10	-PP0	TOLL BRIDGE 52 J Payne 9-10-0	Mr S Mulcaire	--

3-1 Evening Rain, 7-2 Agra, 5-1 Golden Opal, Prudent Peggy, 6-1 Sovereign Niche, 7-1 Full Shilling, 12-1 Martin's Friend, 14-1 others.

3.00 BET WITH THE TOTE NOVICES CHASE (Qualifier: £3,201: 3m 2f 110yd) (5)

1	1124	COURT MELODY 9 (B,CD,G,S) P Nicholls 8-11-12	P Hide	78
2	-214	BEAUREPAIRE 18 (D,BF,S) R Alner 8-11-5	S McNeill	65
3	0	BOHEMIAN HARMONY 38 Miss C Johnsey 6-10-12	G Hogan (3)	--
4	F32F	MOBILE MESSENGER 18 (S) T George 8-10-12	D Bridgwater	77
5	/1-2	SISTER STEPHANIE 17 (G,S) Mrs M McCourt 7-10-7	R Dunwoody	99

5-4 Court Melody, 11-8 Sister Stephanie, 5-1 Beaurepaire, 8-1 Mobile Messenger, 25-1 Bohemian Harmony.

3.30 PLYMOUTH HANDICAP HURDLE (£2,814: 3m 3f) (11 runners)

1	2140	KARAR 9 (F,G,S) R Rowe 6-11-10	D O'Sullivan	98
2	-P2F	THE BOILER WHITE 46 (F,S) T Thomson Jones 8-11-6	G McCourt	89
3	6026	JADIDH 7 (C,F,G,S) C Wildman 8-11-5	D Salter (5)	94
4	FFR0	BETTER BYTHE GLASS 3 (S) N Twiston-Davies 7-11-3	C Maude	86
5	3-40	SNOWY LANE 7 (B,G,S) J Neville 8-11-2	D Gallagher	82
6	1-20	PRINCE OF SALERNO 51 (S) N Gaselee 9-11-1	C Llewellyn	95
7	4/P	SEA PATROL 7 (B,F) M Pipe 9-10-11	Jamie Evans	--
8	P-01	MONTAGNARD 42 (C,G,S) M Bradstock 12-10-10	P Holley	99
9	4663	THE MINDER 18 (S) G Edwards 9-10-7	R Dunwoody	96
10	2-35	ST VILLE 42 (D,G,S) R Buckler 10-10-5	B Powell	91
11	3-P5	IT'S NOT MY FAULT 17 (G,S) P Jones 8-10-0	Mr J Culloty (7)	94

7-2 The Minder, 5-1 Montagnard, 6-1 Prince of Salerno, 7-1 Karar, Sea Patrol, 8-1 Better Bythe Glass, 10-1 Jadidh, 12-1 others.

4.00 EXETER HANDICAP CHASE (£3,765: 2m 5f 110yd) (9)

1	-P1P	TERAO 9 (S) M Pipe 10-12-0	D Bridgwater	99
2	-P5P	JAILBREAKER 11 (C,G,S) B Millman 9-11-3	D Salter (5)	98
3	0432	SUPER TACTICS 17 (G,S) R Alner 8-11-2	Mr P Henley (5)	96
4	6-3U	KINGS CHERRY 9 (S) R Buckler 8-10-12	Mr G Baines (7)	--
5	1F14	BRAMBLEHILL BUCK 13 (B,CD,S) P Nicholls 7-10-10	R Dunwoody	94
6	23P-	POP SONG 271 (CD,F,G,S) G Roe 12-10-9	J Railton	97
7	/R6	MAPLE DANCER 42 (F,G) D Barons 10-10-7	Mr G Shenkin (7)	--
8	552U	SCOTONI 7 (F,G,S) R O'Sullivan 10-10-5	D O'Sullivan	93
9	3542	CLEAR IDEA 42 (CD,F,G) R Frost 8-10-2	J Frost	94

STRATEGY 13:

Travelling Jockeys

Those fortunate and wise enough to attend race meetings are able to gain access to information on jockey bookings that may be denied stay-at-home backers – a fact that was brought home to me most forcibly one May Day Bank Holiday at Warwick. What happened was that when the runners for the fourth race were being prepared, a helicopter deposited Richard Hills in the centre of the track, thus obliging him to sprint to the weighing room. Clearly, here was a man on a mission! Indeed, rapid scrutiny of my racing newspaper revealed that he had tarried at Kempton until 2.40 pm to ride Hamdan al Maktoum's Mubdi (backed down to 10–1 from 12–1) into second place in a seven furlong handicap. I thus concluded that he must have taken off from the day's major meeting at around 3.00 pm and here he was arriving at lowly Warwick to take some more mounts for the same millionaire Arab owner in the last three races on this Midlands card. Astonishingly, all three duly won at 6–1, 9–2 and 7–2.

There is yet another 'dark secret' I have identified when investigating travelling jockeys. It involves capitalising on the fact that a top-flight jockey may travel to a minor meeting for just a few outside rides. If, when doing so, he travels an extensive distance from where he rode on the previous racing day the hint should be taken. So when I noticed that the highly skilled Michael Roberts was due to ride again at lowly Warwick on a Bank Holiday Monday, instead of a more prestigious venue, I felt his journey to the Midlands was likely to be rewarded. I was proved correct when he brought home three Warwick winners – Bestow at 11–4, Haunting Obsession at 13–8 and Capala at 6–5, and when he was also associated with two placed runners – Keen Melody second at 12–1, and Port Vauban third at 2–1!

WARWICK

ROBIN GOODFELLOW	GIMCRACK
2.00 Lady Chaloner	**2.00 Choir Practice**
2.30 Ile De Reine	**2.30 Lady Westown**
3.00 Rio Tejo	**3.00 Rio Tejo**
3.30 Keen Melody	**3.30 Cee-Jay-Ay**
4.00 Into The Future	**4.00 Bundle Of Luck**
4.30 Port Vauban	**4.30 Rhein Legend**
5.00 Chapala	**5.00 Chapala**

FIVE-YEAR RECORD

Jockeys: W Carson 21, S Cauthen 20, Pat Eddery 19, T Quinn 18, J Williams 14.

Trainers: J Berry 17, H Cecil 16, J Dunlop 14, B Hills 13, P Cole 12, G H Price 11, M Stoute 11.

GOING: Good to firm. STALLS: Inside. DRAW ADVANTAGE: Low numbers are favoured in 5f races except when the ground is soft.

2.00 — GAYDON MAIDEN SPRINT STAKES £3,000 (£2,060.00) 5f (13)

1	(8)	054	**CHOIR PRACTICE 11**	H Candy 3-8-11	**S Dawson**	●78
2	(5)	00-5343	**COMEDY RIVER 6**	J Spearing 3-8-11	**E Husband (7)**	68
3	(10)	60250-0	**GUARANTEE 11**	C Austin 3-8-11	**R Wernham**	55
4	(9)	4-0055	**MORPICK 26**	J Leigh 3-8-11	**A Shoults**	57
5	(6)	553200	**RED PIPPIN 13 (B)**	Mrs N Macauley 3-8-11	**N Adams**	71
6	(12)	0	**VILCOE BAY 14**	B McMahon 3-8-11	**P Hill**	—
7	(4)	0/000	**LADY CHALONER 19**	B McMahon 4-8-9	**Ron Hillis (3)**	—
8	(2)	000000	**RUN FOR JOYCE 10**	J Balding 4-8-9	——	—
9	(13)	002435	**BARONESS GYMCRAK 11**	M H Easterby 3-8-6	**P Burke**	70
10	(3)	030-600	**BUFFS EXPRESS 59**	W Wightman 3-8-6	**M Roberts**	71
11	(7)		**QUATRE FEMME**	M Johnston 3-8-6	**A Proud**	—
12	(1)	5-0	**STOCKTINA 98**	L Cottrell 3-8-6	**G Baxter**	—
13	(11)	5	**STORM ORPHAN 41**	G Lewis 3-8-6	**S O'Gorman (5)**	—

Probable SP: 6-4 Choir Practice, 3 Baroness Gymcrak, 5 Buffs Express, 6 Red Pippin, 8 Comedy River. **FAVOURITES: 3 0 1 2 3 1 1.**

1989: Catalani 4 8 4 (M Tebbutt) 15-8 fav W Jarvis 14 ran.

2.30 — WARWICK CESAREWITCH HANDICAP £4,000 added (£3,366.00) 2m (6)

1 (1) 4/06223 **DEBBIE HARRY 30** P Cole 4-9-10 ......**S O'Gorman (5)** **76**
2 (5) 022143 **DALBY DANCER 9 (C3D)** B McMahon 6-9-9 **Ron Hillis (3)** **77**
3 (3) 040-120 **ILE DE REINE 11 (C)** H Candy 4-9-3 ....**S Dawson** **74**
4 (6) 65-2221 **BESTOW 25** B Hills 3-8-10 ....**M Roberts** **70**
5 (4) 135-611 **LADY WESTOWN 11 (D3)** R Holder 6-8-6 ...**N Adams** **●78**
6 (2) 0-00 **LET FLY 131** G Wragg 3-8-6 ....**P D'Arcy** **—**

Probable SP: 9-4 Dalby Dancer, 11-4 Ile de Reine, 4 Lady Westown, 13-2 Debbie Harry, 12 Let Fly. **FAVOURITES: — — — — 0 0 2.**

1989: Lucky Verdict 3 8 11 (Paul Eddery) 100-30 J W Hills 6 ran.

3.00 — HARBURY FILLIES GRADUATION GUARANTEED (2-Y-O) £2,060 5f (7)

1 (4) 230120 **PRINCESS WHO 27 (D)** M McCormack 9-4 ..**G Baxter** **68**
2 (5) 331 **RIO TEJO 33 (D)** J Gosden 9-4.......................**G Brown** **77**
3 (7) 40 **DIVINE BREEZE 34** D Murray-Smith 8-8.......**N Adams** **53**
4 (3) 2 **HAUNTING OBSESSION 9** J Etherington 8-8 **M Roberts** **●78**
5 (1) 23233 **LATIN MASS 66 (BF)** J Berry 8-8 ....**A Shoults** **67**
6 (6) 0 **MISS MARTINA 10** I Balding 8-8 ....**S O'Gorman (5)** **68**
7 (2) 0 **SHADES OF VERA 26** G Lewis 8-8..........**R Wernham** **66**

Probable SP: 11-10 Rio Tejo, 5-2 Miss Martina, 5 Haunting Obsession, 10 Shades Of Vera, 12 Latin Mass. **FAVOURITES: 1 2 2 0 1 3 1.**

1989: Tadwin 2 8 8 (G Baxter) 1-2 fav P T Walwyn 10 ran.

3.30 — WARWICK LADIES LIFEBOAT GUILD HANDICAP (3-Y-O) £3,000 added (£2,973.00) 7f (13)

1 (6) 205050 **KING'S SHILLING 19** I Balding 9-7 .....**S O'Gorman (5)** **76**
2 (4) 021111 **CEE-JAY-AY 11 (C&DCD2)** J Berry 9-7 **S Haworth (7)** **77**
3 (10) 540023 **SUPREME DANCER 20 (BF2)** W Jarvis 9-0 **DOUBTFUL**
4 (8) 4-26 **GOLDEN LOFT 16** D Murray-Smith 8-13...**R Wernham** **71**
5 (2) 066-66 **KEEN MELODY 76** R Hannon 8-11 ....**M Roberts** **65**
6 (5) 60-0066 **PLIE 13** D Arbuthnot 8-10 ....**A Procter (7)** **70**
7 (11) 0-6040 **HEARTHRUG 25** P Walwyn 8-10 ....**K Rutter (7)** **73**
8 (7) 340005 **ABLE ROCKET 41** Mrs N Macauley 8-9 ....**N Adams** **69**
9 (12) 055030 **ROUSKI 25** J Payne 8-8 ....**A Proud** **73**
10 (3) 306002 **SOCKEM 3 (C&DD)** C Williams 8-7 ....**G Baxter** **75**
11 (13) 000635 **NICQUITA 12 (V)** C Elsey 8-6 ....**J Hunter (7)** **70**
12 (1) 545050 **SLEEPLINE PALACE 11 (B)** M Channon 8-1 **A Shoults** **75**
13 (9) 300043 **RACECALL GOLD CARD 19** M McCormack 7-11 **S Dawson** **●78**

Probable SP: 6-4 Cee-Jay-Ay, 3 King's Shilling, 4 Sockem, 5 Sleepline Palace, 8 Keen Melody. **FAVOURITES: — — 2 1 1 0 0.**

1989: Better Now 3 8 6 (P Brette) 9-1 J Etherington 15 ran.

4.00 — ST NICHOLAS SELLING HANDICAP £3,000 added (£2,973.00) 1m 2f 170yds (20)

1 (7) 461432 **MYSTERY BAND 7 (J)(C&DBF)** C Beever 4-9-11 **K Rutter (7)** **68**
2 (20) 6-02004 **CHART CROSS 9** K Bridgwater 4-9-3 ....**P D'Arcy** **69**
3 (18) 0/04655 **SELEUCIA 12** M O'Neill 5-9-0.............................**——** **●78**
4 (19) 550035 **CHANDANNE 9** T Casey 3-8-10..................**D McKay** **66**
5 (5) 5130-54 **JEALOUS LOVER 28 (B)** P Makin 6-8-9 ...**T Sprake (5)** **76**
6 (17) 00-00 **SHAHRIZA 51** C Elsey 3-8-9 ....**J Hunter (7)** **—**
7 (4) 0000-05 **ORDER OF MERIT 34** J White 5-8-8.................**——** **70**
8 (8) 250045 **BUNDLE OF LUCK 6 (B)** Lord John FitzGerald 3-8-7 **M Roberts** **—**
9 (14) 00-0034 **POMME D'AMOUR 31 (V)(BF)** N Graham 3-8-6 **G Baxter** **72**
10 (10) 034025- **HEADBEE 293** K White 4-8-6 ....**A Shoults** **66**
11 (13) 000540 **DARAROYAL 3 (B)** Mrs N Macauley 3-8-5 **R Wernham** **60**
12 (1) 05/6046 **HAND PAINTED 17** J Pearce 6-8-4...............**G Austin** **70**
13 (9) 003454 **INTO THE FUTURE 9** A Stringer 3-8-2..........**P Burke** **72**
14 (2) 00-0060 **NORABLASSIE 13** H Collingridge 3-8-2............**——** **63**
15 (6) 00000-0 **HATAY 38 (B)** P Blockley 5-8-1 ....**A Proud** **—**
16 (12) 00-0001 **WEEK ST MARY 13** R Hodges 4-7-13 ....**N Adams** **70**
17 (15) 0-40000 **CORINTHIAN GIRL 27 (B)** R Dickin 3-7-12 **S Dawson** **65**
18 (3) 0-00000 **KINGSMERE 34** R Hannon 3-7-10 .....**S O'Gorman (5)** **—**

19 (11) 606000 **BILLAN TARA 11** C Booth 4-7-8 ....—— —
20 (16) 03000/ **TIMMY BOY 1132** J Smith 10-7-7 ....—— —

Probable SP: 7-2 Week St. Mary, 9-2 Jealous Lover, 5 Bundle Of Luck, 13-2 Mystery Band, 8 Order Of Merit, 10 Into The Future, 12 Hand Painted, 14 Pomme d'Amour. **FAVOURITES: — — 2 2 0 0 1.**

1989: Verbarium 9 9 7 (M A Giles) 9-4 fav Mrs J R Ramsden 20 ran.

4.30 — PINLEY NURSERY (2-Y-O Handicap) £3,500 added (£3,003.00) 1m (9)

1 (8) 015421 **PORT VAUBAN 14** R Hannon 9-7 ....**M Roberts 70**
2 (6) 054 **FIERCE 13** J Jenkins 9-2 ....—— **65**
3 (7) 01 **TOREL 18** J Dunlop 8-10 ....**R Wernham 68**
4 (9) 405 **AMBASSADOR ROYALE 44** P Cole 8-9 ....**G Baxter 65**
5 (5) 00635 **HIGHLAND MEETING 14** H Candy 8-9.......**S Dawson 70**
6 (1) 216542 **BOLD SPARK 9** J Berry 7-12 ....**A Shoults 72**
7 (3) 65533 **GYMCRAK FORTUNE 16 (BF)** M H Easterby 7-12
P Burke 66
8 (2) 03062 **RHEIN LEGEND 14** J Watts 7-10 ....**N Adams ●78**
9 (4) 330330 **VITTORIA GLENN 19** R Holder 7-8................**A Proud 71**

Probable SP: 15-8 Torel, 11-4 Ambassador Royale, 4 Port Vauban, 6 Rhein Legend, 8 Bold Spark. **FAVOURITES: 1 0 1 1 1 0 1.**

1989: Marasol 2 9 4 (Paul Eddery) 9-2 jt fav J L Dunlop 8 ran.

5.00 — BARFORD MAIDEN FILLIES' GUARANTEED SWEEPSTAKES (3-Y-O) £3,000 (£2,060.00) 1m (8)

1 (3) 0- **AGAINST THE FLOW 345** J Czerpak 8-11 ..**N Adams** —
2 (1) 3 **CHAPALA 14** A Stewart 8-11.....................**M Roberts 73**
3 (7) 4545 **CHOIR LEADER 41** B Hanbury 8-11 ....**A Shoults ●78**
4 (2) 0-43242 **FAIRY FORTUNE 9 (V)(BF3)** I Balding 8-11
S O'Gorman (5) 77
5 (8) 000-03 **NORSTOCK 26** J White 8-11....................**K Rutter (7) 64**
6 (4) 0-6 **PRESSED FOR TIME 17** M O'Neill 8-11 ....—— —
7 (5) **PURSUIT** C Austin 8-11...........................**R Wernham** —
8 (6) **SPORTING LASS** J Berry 8-11 ....**G Baxter** —

Probable SP: 7-4 Fairy Fortune, 9-4 Chapala, 4 Choir Leader, 8 Sporting Lass, 10 Norstock, 14 Pursuit. **FAVOURITES: 0 0 2 0 2 0 1.**

1989: Mountain Bluebird 3 8 11 (B Rouse) 5-4 fav W R Hern 10 ran.

NEWMARKET (Craven) — 2.30 Let Fly. 3.00 Rio Tejo. 4.00 Pomme d'Amour. 5.00 Choir Leader.

NORTHERNER — 3.00 Haunting Obsession. 3.30 Cee-Jay-Ay. 4.30 Rhein Legend. 5.00 Sporting Lass.

BLINKERED (OR VISORED) FIRST TIME: 3.30 Nicquita, Sleepline Palace. 4.00 Bundle of Luck. 5.00 Fairy Fortune.

WARWICK Firm

2.00 (5f) — **CHOIR PRACTICE** (S Dawson) **5-2** fav, 1; **Quatre Femme 10-1**, 2; **Comedy River 7-1**, 3. **13 Ran.** (H Candy, Wantage). 2½, nk. **Tote:** £3.50; £1.70, £4.80, £1.60. **DF:** £49.00. **CSF:** £28.59.

2.30 (2m h'cap) — **BESTOW** (M Roberts) **11-4**, 1; **Let Fly 20-1**, 2; **Lady Westown 15-8 fav**, 3. **6 Ran.** (B Hills, Manton). 2½, ¾. **Tote:** £3.40; £2.00, £3.00. **DF:** £19.30. **CSF:** £37.67.

3.00 (5f) — **HAUNTING OBSESSION** (M Roberts) **13-8**, 1; **Princess Who 16-1**, 2; **Miss Martina 15-2**, 3. **7 Ran.** 11-8 Fav Rio Tejo. (J Etherington, Malton). ½, 1. **Tote:** £2.80; £1.70, £3.90. **DF:** £14.40. **CSF:** £22.43.

3.30 (7f h'cap) — **NICQUITA** (J Hunter) **16-1**, 1; **Keen Melody 12-1**, 2; **Cee-Jay-Ay 11-4**, 3. **12** ran. 5-2 fav Sockem. (C Elsey, Lambourn). 2½, 1. **Tote:** £15.60; £3.30, £2.70, £1.60. **DF:** £174.40. **CSF:** £165.49. **Tricast:** £622.11. NR: Supreme Dancer.

4.00 (1m 2f 170yd S h'cap) — **SELEUCIA** (M O'Reilly) **14-1**, 1; **Hand Painted 10-1**, 2; **Corinthian Girl 25-1**, 3; **Into The Future 8-1**, 4. **19** ran. 11-2 Fav Pomme D'Amour. (M O'Neill, Lydiate). 1½, 1½. **Tote:** £37.20; £6.60, £2.90, £9.40, £1.80. **DF:** £120.70. **CSF:** £137.92. **Tricast:** £3,146.28. **NR:** Bundle Of Luck.

4.30 (1m h'cap) — **RHEIN LEGEND** (N Adams) **7-2**, 1; **Highland Meeting 12-1**, 2; **Port Vauban 2-1** fav, 3. **9 Ran.** (J Watts, Richmond). ½, 1. **Tote:** £5.10; £1.80, £2.60, £1.50. **DF:** £19.40. **CSF:** £41.17. **Tricast:** £97.55.

PART THREE: EXPLOITING RACEDAY FACTORS

STRATEGY 14:

Making the Going Easier

A very surprising omission from an otherwise very soundly based method of form assessment by computer is any consideration of the going which, during one Royal Ascot meeting, for example, made something of a nonsense of the form book. Interestingly, those subscribing to currently fashionable catastrophe theories might well attribute the frequent successes of long-priced horses on heavy or soft ground to the 'hysteresis' effect occasioned by the change to such extreme ground conditions from the sounder surfaces that are often found on British racecourses and on which form tends to work out far more readily.

The fact is that few horses are truly at home in mud or really relish soft ground conditions and, if you know their names, you will be at a considerable advantage when there is a cut in the ground. A little homework is, of course, necessary here, but all the information required will be found conveniently to hand in the form summaries contained in a racing daily and even *The Times*, by means of the symbols G, S and F, indicates the good, soft or firm ground on which past winners have prevailed, even though these abbreviations are, of course, blanket terms that embrace going that may actually have been heavy, good to soft ('yielding' in Ireland), good to firm, firm to hard!

Once again I would recommend studying *Raceform Notebook's* invaluable 'Index to Winners' feature. This gives details of the ground conditions on which past winners have scored and, most usefully, indicates over what distances and tracks these successes were gained. Perhaps the 'darkest secret' regarding the going is that when it features true extremes – in other words when it is heavy or hard – you will be wise to concentrate attention on the few contestants that have previously won on such demanding terrain. For example, when some time ago the going was heavy at my local course at Stratford-upon-Avon, it seemed wise to concentrate on the claims of those few runners that had previously won in the mud. These were a 5–6 winner in the main chase on the card and two mudlarks that opposed each other in another chase. In a third such race, this was the fate of two other runners while two more contested the handicap hurdle that concluded this Stratford card. In two of these three races, the market proved a most reliable guide as victory went either to the favourite or to the qualifier that started at a much shorter price than its rival.

This is not to say, however, that all horses which again triumph in the mud start at short prices. Indeed, their frequent successes at long odds owe much to the fact that their form lines are marred by many 'ducks' eggs' which delude many into thinking they are unreliable. Form figures such as 020001002, for example, could mean that when the horse in question rather rarely encountered the cut in the ground it appreciated, it was second, then won and finally finished second again at good odds, since by then many believed it had 'gone off' or was out of form.

Research has shown that, as might be expected, horses of proven stamina like Little Polveir, the 1989 Grand National winner, that carry lightish weights over the heavy or soft ground on which they have previously prevailed, often win highly competitive long-distance races at long odds that fail to reflect the fact that, prior to these victories, they ran on unsuitably good or firm ground. Indeed, when you notice that the going has suddenly changed from such terrain to soft, or preferably heavy, ground, it is time to try to predict precisely which horse seems capable of causing a form upset or 'catastrophe' in a long-distance event, during which many contestants, especially if they have to carry high weights, will become well and truly 'bogged down'. This is why in the 1989 National I plumped for Little Polveir since he was quite lowly weighted, was at a decent price of 28–1 that befitted a 'catastrophe' winner, and had demonstrated his ability to win over a marathon trip on a treacherous surface by previously having won the Scottish Grand National on heavy ground at Ayr. Little Polveir thus looked a 'live' outsider and candidate to spring a surprise; I was delighted when he ran out a ready winner at Aintree.

The most convincing explanation of why some horses produce their best form on sodden ground was once provided by Phil Bull, the former boss of *Timeform* and, until his death, one of racing's best known gurus. According to John Hislop, Bull felt that fluency on soft or heavy ground depends on a horse's weight. Significantly, Little Polveir and Ben Nevis (successful in bottomless National ground at Aintree at 40–1) were both small steeplechasers. Understandably, heavy horses have to exert great effort to pull their feet out of mud, whereas lighter ones may well skim over the top of it. Such an ability naturally has a good deal to do with a horse's action. Indeed, a horse with a high-knee, 'round' action is able to pull its feet out of heavy ground far more easily than one with a low 'daisy cutting' action. Such a view was certainly endorsed by former jockey and trainer, Jack Leach, who once commented that horses that 'can go through mud like ducks going home to breakfast are invariably perfect movers'.

Given Bull's insights, I recommend that you check details of a horse's size, weight and action from *Timeform* publications to see whether it has the weight and action to give it an advantage in the mud. While you wisely scrutinise *Timeform's* description of a horse's conformation, it may also pay to remember that some judges argue that horses with little 'donkey' feet tend to become stuck in the mud, while those with large policemen's feet can happily splash along on top of it. This view was certainly vindicated by the racing performances of the colt Streetfighter some seasons ago when his large 'plates of meat' certainly seemed to give him a distinct 'edge' when there was give in the ground.

My final tip for when the heavens have opened sufficiently to really water the track concerns the fact that on such occasions some trainers will spare no expense to find a race run on going that suits their charges. For example, Sigwells Miss once so impressed her trainer, Bill Turner, when he worked her in desperately boggy ground on his training gallops in Dorset that he sent her on an 800-mile round trip to Hamilton where, on very heavy ground, he landed a wager of £1,000 at 6–1, as well as the Zarewitch Vodka Selling Stakes by no less than three lengths!

Understandably too, the concrete-like terrain that seems even more likely to be found on British racecourses, as our summers become yet more tropical, confers certain advantages on some very different performers. Here I am not just talking of the proven ability of that minority of racehorses to act on firm, or preferably hard, ground, or the belief that even fewer racehorses love the sound of their rattling feet, but of the fact that a high weight is obviously unable to cause these particular parts of the equine anatomy to become disadvantageously bogged down when the ground on which they race is crying out for water. Indeed, a glance at lists of record times shows that many of these were set by horses that humped heavy weights to victory when running on firm or hard ground.

What I suggest you should do when the going is officially shown as 'good to firm' or even better as 'firm' or 'hard' is first to select sprint races on the flat and two mile hurdles and steeplechases over the sticks. Second, I suggest you pay careful attention to the claims of those whose past form has been good enough to ensure that they are highly weighted. As for highly weighted two-year-olds running on firm ground, it may well pay to check to see whether they were foaled early enough to suggest they are sufficiently strong and well-developed to carry high weights to victory in nurseries. For example, I once watched a Barry Hills trained two-year-old register a weight defying victory on firm ground in a five furlong nursery at a Warwick night meeting. One of the main reasons I backed him was that my *Racing Post* revealed that he was a colt with a relatively early (February 10th) foaling date and my belief that he was thus physically mature enough to defy a 'steadier' of 9st was confirmed by his imposing appearance in the paddock. I was not really surprised when this young colt registered a facile victory. As for older sprinters, the many rapidly successive victories of several of trainer David Chapman's older 'pigeon catchers' have also suggested that top weights can also be unbeatable on the firm, provided you already fancy them on the strength of recent very good form.

STRATEGY 15:

Courses for Horses

The fact that the topography of racecourses presents some runners with major advantages, and seriously disadvantages others, was spectacularly demonstrated by the defeat of Desert Orchid in the 1990 Gold Cup at Cheltenham, a course whose left-hand configuration and testing undulating terrain he found so radically different from the right-handed 'park' courses on which he had registered so many triumphs. I realise, of course, that Britain's best-loved steeplechaser did win the 1989 Gold Cup, but this victory and gallant display followed the tragic fall of his main rival, Ten Plus.

Since most racecourses are left-handed – a configuration that most racehorses seem more comfortable with – for much of the time only a few runners are inconvenienced by the direction in which they are asked to run. However, if long-distance events are run over furlong after furlong of ground that frequently turns to the right, as in long-distance steeplechases, it is likely that only a few of the horses contesting them will relish their task. The secret then, when you are assessing form for races run on right-handed tracks, is to concentrate your attention on horses whose past victories show they can more than cope with having to race the 'wrong way' round.

Indeed, that some runners may have had divine assistance in performing such a freakish 'miracle' is perhaps suggested by the many victories at right-handed Huntingdon of French Saint, at Ludlow of Cardinal's Outburst and at Perth of Father Delaney! Perhaps the best way of exploiting the 'right-handed courses for horses' plan is to back a multiple course winner in a race run over a sizeable distance of ground over a National Hunt track.

STRATEGY 16:

The Luck of the Draw

The draw for places in the starting stalls is clearly of little importance in races of two miles or more that, in modern times, are fairly rarely seen on British racecourses, but, on certain tracks, in many shorter races run on particular going, and when the stalls are in certain positions, it can have crucial effects on the outcomes of races. Indeed, Dick Whitford, whose highly accurate private handicap ratings once led bookmaker William Hill to induce him to run his form room, used to warn his *Sporting Life* readers that his figures took no account of this crucial raceday factor.

It has been estimated that at Sandown, if a sprint race is run on soft going and the stalls are placed on the far side, high drawn horses have as much as a 1lb advantage per stall, so a runner allotted the number 15 berth would have as much as 10lb in hand over a rival drawn 5 – a margin which in events over a short distance would be equivalent to over three lengths!

The following chart which I have compiled details the circumstances in which the backer would be especially wise to concentrate his attention on well-drawn contenders.

WHITE'S DRAW RATING

Racecourse	Distance of Race	Going	Position of Stalls	Draw Advantage in Units
Ayr	5 Furlongs	Any	Far Side	XXX to Low Drawn Runners
Ayr	6 Furlongs	Any	Far Side	XXX to Low Drawn Runners
Beverley	5 Furlongs	Any	Far Side	XXX to High Drawn Runners
Beverley	6 Furlongs	Any	Far Side	XXX to High Drawn Runners
Edinburgh	5 Furlongs	Any	Stands Side	XXXX to Low Drawn Runners
Edinburgh	7 Furlongs	Any	Immaterial	XXX to High Drawn Runners
Edinburgh	8 Furlongs	Any	Immaterial	XXX to High Drawn Runners
Epsom	5 Furlongs	Any	Immaterial	XXX to High Drawn Runners
Epsom	8+ Furlongs	Any	Immaterial	XXXX to Low Drawn Runners
Epsom	10 Furlongs	Any	Immaterial	XXXX to Low Drawn Runners
Folkestone	10 Furlongs	Any	Immaterial	XXXX to Low Drawn Runners
Folkestone	12 Furlongs	Any	Immaterial	XXXX to High Drawn Runners
Goodwood	7 Furlongs	Any	Immaterial	XXX to High Drawn Runners
Goodwood	8 Furlongs	Any	Immaterial	XXX to High Drawn Runners

Kempton	5 Furlongs	Any	Stands Side	XXX to Low Drawn Runners
Kempton	6 Furlongs	Any	Stands Side	XXX to Low Drawn Runners
Kempton	5 Furlongs	Any	Far Side	XXX to High Drawn Runners
Kempton	6 Furlongs	Any	Far Side	XXX to High Drawn Runners
Newcastle	5 Furlongs	Soft	Centre or Far Side	XXX to Low Drawn Runners
Newcastle	6 Furlongs	Soft	Centre or Far Side	XXX to Low Drawn Runners
Newcastle	7 Furlongs	Soft	Centre or Far Side	XXX to Low Drawn Runners
Nottingham	5 Furlongs	Soft	Stands Side	XXX to High Drawn Runners
Nottingham	6 Furlongs	Soft	Stands Side	XXX to High Drawn Runners
Sandown	5 Furlongs	Good or Firm	Far Side	XXX to High Drawn Runners
Sandown	5 Furlongs	Soft	Far Side	XXXXXXXXXX to High Drawn Runners
Thirsk	5 Furlongs	Soft	Stands Side	XXXXXXXXXX to High Drawn Runners
Thirsk	6 Furlongs	Soft	Stands Side	XXXXXXXXXX To High Drawn Runners
York	5 Furlongs	Any	Stands Side	XXX to Low Drawn Runners
York	6 Furlongs	Any	Stands Side	XXX to Low Drawn Runners

As it happens, if a horse is top-rated according to a private handicap whose scale corresponds with the official Jockey Club handicap – of 0–140 (0–10st) for Flat racing and 0–175 (0–12st) for National Hunt races – any further superiority the draw may give it over its rivals can be calculated. Since both 'Postmark' and 'Topspeed' – the respective form and time private handicappers whose ratings appear in the *Racing Post* – work to these scales, one 'secret' way I have of ensuring I get an 'edge' in my betting on contests mentioned in the above draw table is to back any runner top-rated by both these experts that this table shows also has a favourable draw on its side. This is because such an animal can be said on three objective and numerically based sets of figures (based on its form, previous race times and the position allotted it in the stalls) to have many points in its favour. You will not be able to spot such a runner every day but if you do find one it should have an outstanding chance of making the frame.

This was certainly the case with some particularly well-drawn horses at Thirsk when, as was reported in the *Daily Star's* annual racing guide, one 'particularly shrewd investor' landed a quarter of a million pound payout by perming the four highest drawn runners in a sprint run on soft going. He was one of the few to realise that at Thirsk, as the *Daily Star* put it, 'the benefit of the better surface near the stands side rail only extends to a narrow width of ground and so only those with the very highest numbers are likely to benefit'. This truly 'dark secret' of the turf is certainly vindicated by the following complete set of results for sprint races run on the soft at Thirsk not so long ago.

The results reproduced represent a most impressive vindication of the 'draw for horses' approach. Races 221 and 4063 provided particularly impressive results and, of the 15 opportunities for places presented by the above five events, no less than 11 went to highly drawn runners, while in three of the five races, victory went to the highest drawn runners at odds of 11–4, 2–5 and 11–2! Indeed, the race-reader's comment against Gemini Fire – 'made all stands side' – could hardly be bettered as a vindication of one particular entry in the above draw table. Horses well rated on form and time in the *Racing Post* that this table shows as having been allotted a really favourable draw are definitely those to include in your forecast and tricast wagers, preferably the former since bookmakers are now reducing dividends on the latter wager if they feel the influence of the draw is really crucial. They must have read this chapter in this book's first edition!

THIRSK (soft)
Friday April 14th

Going Correction: PLUS 0.75 sec. per fur. (races 1,2,4), PLUS 0.55 (3,5,6)

221 EBF Briton Maiden Stakes (2-y-o) £2,700 5f.................(2:30)

95^{2} CHAMPAGNE GOLD 9-0 T Ives (13) *dsptd ld, shwd ahead frm hfwy, rdn and kpt on wl fnl furlong*..(11 to 4 op 5 to 2 tchd 3 to 1) 1

WANDA 8-9 W Ryan (1) *sluggish strt, gd hdwy on outsd to chal fnl furlong, ran on*..........(33 to 1) 2

SHERIFF'S BAND 9-0 M Birch (12) *improved frm midfield o'r one furlong out, ran green and not quicken*............(7 to 1 op 4 to 1) 3

66^{2} SINK THE FLEET (USA) 9-0 K Darley (11) *broke fst, swtchd to ld on stands side at hfwy, rdn and no extr o'r one furlong out.* ....(5 to 2 fav op 4 to 1) 4

66^{5} PREMIER DEVELOPER 9-0 D Nicholls (6) *gd speed centre, drvn alng and no extr o'r one furlong out*.............(20 to 1 op 14 to 1) 5

47^{2} TENDERLOIN 9-0 Kim Tinkler (7) *tucked away in midfield, nvr plcd to chal*..........................(33 to 1) 6

95 REEF WIND 9-0 J Lowe (14) *missed break, chsd alng thrght, nvr nr to chal*..........................(10 to 1 op 16 to 1) 7

53^{5} LUNA PROBE 8-9 J H Brown (10) *speed till wknd und pres o'r one furlong out*..........................(14 to 1 op 10 to 1) 8

EL ARAB 9-0 G Duffield (8) *outpcd*..............(25 to 1 op 20 to 1) 9

88^{4} BLUE BELL RIBBONS (bl) 9-0 J Carroll (5) *broke wl to race wth ldrs for 3 fs, sn btn*..........................(7 to 1 op 4 to 1) 10

HAPPY VISION 8-9 (5*) Julie Bowker (2) *slow into strd, al outpcd.* ....(33 to 1) 11

VINEGAR BOB 9-0 M Wigham (3) *slow into strd, al beh*.... (33 to 1) 12

JENNY B QUICK 8-9 Dean McKeown (9) *early speed, rdn and outpcd frm hfwy*..........................(33 to 1) 13

Dist: ½l, 2l, 1½l, 2½l, 2½l, 2½l, sht-hd. 1m 4.50s. a 7.00s (13 Ran).

SR: 35/28/25/19/9/-/ (Mrs Claire Massey), Denys Smith

222 Knayton Selling Stakes (3-y-o) £1,688 6f..................... (3:00)

97 EASTERN EMBER (bl) 8-11 G Duffield (14) *fst away, made all and* [illegible]........................(6 to 1 op 6 to 1 tchd 5 to 1) 1

REMWOOD GIRL 8-11 T Ives (5) *chsd ldrs on outsd, drvn and ran on wl ins fnl furlong*..........................(20 to 1) 2

89^{9} MEDF[illegible] (USA) 8-11 M McAndrew (11) *patiently rdn, steady hdwy* [illegible] *shaken up o'r one furlong out, fnshd wl*......(6 to 1 op 9 to 2) 3

CRAKAFU 9-6 M Birch (3) *nvr far away, bustled alng last 2 fs, styd on*..........................(6 to 1 op 4 to 1) 4

MADONNINA 8-11 M Fry (8) *chsd ldg bunch, drvn and kpt on one pace fnl furlong*.......................... (20 to 1) 5

EMPRESS NICKI 8-11 N Day (20) *gd speed stands side for o'r 4 fs.* ....(10 to 1 op 8 to 1) 6

SPS CREATIVE 8-11 M Wigham (9) *al chasing ldrs, bustled alng 2 fs out, no imprsn*..........................(10 to 1) 7

VAIGLY KATE 8-11 W Ryan (1) *patiently rdn, steady hdwy last 2 fs, prmsg*..........(7 to 1 op 5 to 1 tchd 8 to 1) 8

89 GIVE ME A DAY 8-11 Dean McKeown (13) *chsd ldg bunch, hrd at work and no imprsn last 2 fs*.......................... (20 to 1) 9

PERT 8-4 (7*) R P Elliott (15) *slow into strd, steady hdwy last 2 fs, improved*..........................(20 to 1) 10

JESTMENOT 9-0 L Charnock (21) *missed break, chsd alng and nvr nr to chal*..........................(20 to 1) 11

145^{9} WELSH FLUTE 8-6 (5*) P Burke (22) *chsd alng in midfield, nvr nr to chal*..........................(16 to 1) 12

REASON TO LAUGH 9-0 S Horsfall (16) *early speed, ran green and lost pl hfwy, eased whn btn*..........................(20 to 1) 13

160^{6} KNOWETOP 8-11 J H Brown (17) *feeling pace and rdn hfwy, btn whn hmpd o'r one furlong out*........(9 to 1 op 7 to 1 tchd 10 to 1) 14

89^{5} RUBINKA 8-6 (5*) S Wood (7) *speed wth chasing grp for 4 fs.* ....(4 to 1 fav op 8 to 1 tchd 7 to 2 and 3 to 1) 15

IMPERIAL FLAME 8-11 S Webster (12) *chsd alng to hold pl aftr 2 fs, wknd hfwy*.......................... (16 to 1 op 14 to 1) 16

158^{9} WYNCKY 9-0 D Nicholls (10) *chsd alng hfwy, sn btn*.........(16 to 1) 17

BIRD BATH 8-11 S Lawes (6) *sn outpcd*.........(12 to 1 op 10 to 1) 18

BIRMINGHAM'S GLORY 8-6 (5*) R Lappin (18) *gd speed wth*

chasing grp till wknd last 2 fs.. (14 to 1) 19
MAKE YOUR PLANS (USA) 9-3 Kim Tinkler (19) *al beh, tld off.*
....(5 to 1 op 4 to 1) 20

Dist: 1½l, ½l, 1½l, 1½l, 1½l, 2½l, ¾l, ¾l, nk, ¾l. 1m 21.30s. a 10.90s (20 Ran).
(Thoroughbred Racing Ltd), M W Easterby

224 Hambleton Graduation Stakes (3-y-o) £1,935 5f..............(4:00)

69^{3} **SPOILT SON 9-0 M Birch (6)** *hng lft thrght, chsd ldr and rdn 2 fs out, ran on to ld fnl furlong.*
.... (5 to 2 on op 11 to 4 on tchd 9 to 4 on and 2 to 1 on) 1
146^{3} **PREVAILING WIND 9-0 M Wigham (1)** *tried to make all, rdn and hdd fnl furlong, one pace*........................ (7 to 1 op 5 to 1) 2
GENTLE HERO (USA) 9-0 K Fallon (2) *missed break, last and outpcd till ran on wl fnl furlong*....................(20 to 1 op 16 to 1) 3
160^{3} **FULHAM TRADER (bl) 9-0 J Carroll (4)** *chsd ldg pair, hrd at work hfwy, no imprsn*.........................(5 to 1 op 4 to 1 tchd 11 to 2) 4
BAR FLY (Fr) 9-0 D Nicholls (3) *flt out the whole way, styd on, nvr dngrs*.. (20 to 1 op 14 to 1) 5
ALWAYS TREASURE 8-11 N Carlisle (5) *sn outpcd, tld off.*
....(25 to 1 op 20 to 1) 6

Dist: 1l, 2l, 1½l, 3l, 15l. 1m 5.30s. a 7.80s (6 Ran).
SR: 18/14/6/-/-/-/ **(Maktoum Al Maktoum), A A Scott**

THIRSK (soft)
Saturday November 11th

Going Correction: PLUS 0.15 sec. per fur. (races 1,2,3,4,6,8), PLUS 0.25 (5,7)

4063 George Farndon Engineering Handicap (0-110) £6,940 5f.. (2:35)

3896^{3} GEMINI FIRE |67| 5-8-1^{1} M Roberts (24) *made all stands side, quickened and ran on strly fnl furlong*..........(11 to 2 op 10 to 1) 1
3918^{3} ROYAL FAN |66| 6-8-0 J Lowe (23) *al wl plcd, effrt and drvn o'r one furlong out, not pace of wnr*..............(3 to 1 fav op 7 to 2) 2
3896 JOE SUGDEN |82| 5-9-2 L Dettori (21) *al hndy, rdn and not quicken appr fnl furlong*............(11 to 1 op 10 to 1 tchd 12 to 1) 3
3896* RESPECTABLE JONES |59| (v) 3-7-7 N Carlisle (18) *drvn to improve frm midfield 2 fs out, ran on finish.*
....(9 to 1 op 7 to 1 tchd 10 to 1) 4
3713^{6} MEESON KAMP |76| 3-8-10 J Carroll (12) *chsd ldrs, ran on frm midfield last 2 fs, nvr nrr*..........................(14 to 1 op 10 to 1) 5
3967^{8} DENSBEN |66| 5-7-7 (7*) P Dalton (15) *drvn alng to go pace, styd on wl ins fnl furlong*.. (10 to 1) 6
3730 SLOE BERRY |70| 3-8-4 G Carter (11) *speed wth ldrs stands side for o'r 3 fs*................................(16 to 1 op 14 to 1) 7
3845^{4} THAT'S THE ONE |88| 3-9-8 A McGlone (8) *chsd alng to improve frm midfield last 2 fs, nrst finish*..................(14 to 1 op 12 to 1) 8
3896^{5} LOFT BOY |65| (bl) 6-7-13^{5} W Carson (2) *wth ldr far side, hrd drvn o'r one furlong out, no extr*......................(14 to 1 op 16 to 1) 9
4045^{3} YEOMAN FORCE |66| (v) 3-7-7 (7*) N Kennedy (5) *improved und pres 2 fs out, not pace to chal*..................(50 to 1 op 33 to 1) 10
3020^{8} CREE BAY |62| 10-7-10^{3} C Rutter (20) *pushed alng and nvr nr to chal*.. (50 to 1) 11
3896^{4} BELLA SEVILLE |60| (bl) 5-7-8 T Williams (9) *chsd ldg pair far side, eased whn btn o'r one furlong out*.......... (16 to 1 op 12 to 1) 12
1030 TEE WALL |59| 3-7-5^{3} (5*) Dale Gibson (16) *chsd alng and nvr trbld ldrs*..(50 to 1) 13
3920 CATALANI |78| 4-8-7 (5*) M Tebbutt (6) *nvr a factor.*
....(25 to 1 op 20 to 1) 14
3896^{9} IMPALA LASS |83| 6-9-3 B Raymond (13) *pressed ldrs stands side till fdd o'r one furlong out*.......... (33 to 1 op 25 to 1) 15
3703^{5} KABCAST |72| 4-7-13 (7*) A Todd (1) *led far side grp, wndrd and wknd quickly last 2 fs*.....................(25 to 1 op 20 to 1) 16
3918 WHIPPER IN |61| 5-7-9 G Bardwell (3) *nvr a factor.*

....(33 to 1 op 25 to 1) 17

3135 GLENCROFT [86] 5-9-6 Dean McKeown (10) *al struggling.* ....(33 to 1 op 25 to 1) 18

3896 J CHEEVER LOOPHOLE [71] 4-8-5 M Birch (17) *nvr shwd wth ch.* ....(14 to 1 op 16 to 1) 19

3918 SULLY'S CHOICE (USA) [76] 8-8-5 (5*) S Wood (19) *nvr got into race*..(20 to 1 op 16 to 1) 20

1837[7] LOVE PRINCE [69] 3-8-3[2] Paul Eddery (14) *outpcd.* .... (20 to 1 tchd 25 to 1) 21

Dist: 4l, 2l, 1½l, 1l, sht-hd, nk, 1l, nk, 1l, ¾l. 1m 0.20s. a 2.70s (21 Ran).
SR: 58/41/49/20/33/22/ (P McMahon), M P Naughton

4065 Remembrance Day EBF Stakes (Listed Race) £7,700 6f... (3:35)

3732 DAWN SUCCESS 3-8-5 M Roberts (11) *nvr far away, drvn ahead entering fnl furlong, ran on*.......... (11 to 2 op 8 to 1 tchd 5 to 1) 1

3844[8] BLYTON LAD 3-9-0 S Webster (9) *al wl plcd, led 2 fs out till entering last, kpt on well*............................ (10 to 1 tchd 11 to 1) 2

3920[8] BAY BAY 3-8-7 J Reid (8) *improved to chal o'r one furlong out, crrd lft and not quicken ins last*..................(16 to 1 op 14 to 1) 3

3920[6] GOLDEN ANCONA 6-8-6 N Day (10) *co'red up in midfield, rng on und pres whn hmpd fnl furlong.* (5 to 1 jt-fav op 11 to 2 tchd 9 to 2) 4

3845[5] PROFILIC 4-8-11 G Carter (13) *drvn up frm midfield o'r one furlong out, veered lft and one pace cl hme*.............(14 to 1 op 20 to 1) 5

3845 SHARP REMINDER 5-8-13 G Baxter (12) *wl plcd on ins, hrd rdn and ev ch o'r one furlong out, no extr.* ....(6 to 1 op 5 to 1 tchd 7 to 1) 6

3920 BE FRESH 3-8-10 L Dettori (4) *led centre for 4 fs, wknd.* ....(6 to 1 op 5 to 1) 7

4019* BREEZED WELL 3-8-10 (5ex) M Tebbutt (2) *bustled alng to keep up hfwy, sn outpcd*................(16 to 1 op 14 to 1 tchd 20 to 1) 8

3920[9] LUNA BID 6-8-11 J Williams (6) *rdn all the way, nvr on terms.* ....(20 to 1 op 16 to 1) 9

3920 KNIGHT OF MERCY 3-8-10 W Carson (1) *chsd alng to go pace hfwy, sn btn*...(16 to 1) 10

STRATEGY 17:

The Fitting of Blinkers

The blinkers of hope and optimism necessarily worn by many owners and trainers may well 'blind' them to the fact that other connections may well have done as much, if not more, to win races. There are, of course, other blinkers that can affect behaviour – those worn by some racehorses! Sometimes wearing these can produce effects that come as pleasant surprises to their connections, but not always to those backers who have been wise enough to anticipate that certain runners sporting blinkers for the very first time may improve on their previous form. This was certainly the case with Balthus, the shock 50–1 winner of the Cambridgeshire. Indeed, it was returned at this long starting price (and a massive 116–1 on the Tote) because most racegoers present at 'Headquarters' were ignorant of the fact that Balthus had worked so well at home in blinkers prior to the big race that his trainer, Jeremy Glover, resolved to let him wear them for the first time on the racecourse, in a bid to capture the first leg of the 'Autumn Double'!

Most daily newspapers and the specialist racing dailies will indicate which horses are due to wear blinkers and which contestants, rather more crucially, are about to do so for the very first time. It is my belief that the latter circumstance can, on occasion, provide particularly clear pointers to possible success especially if the horse in question seems about to improve for other clearly discernible reasons. In general, if a previously unblinkered runner is shown in the *Sporting Life* to be on the upgrade, or is due to race round the right turns of such tracks as Chester, Brighton or Epsom, then it may well run a blinder! Again, if a debutant in the 'shades' is shown by the *Sporting Life's* Flat or National Hunt private handicapper to be superior to its rivals on its form rating of the previous season, with its eyes for once glued to the track, it may be able to re-establish this superiority!

Many newspapers will reveal initially blinkered runners or those in visors, and tables of form ratings in racing dailies will show those that are dropping in class. Alternatively, pre-race form study may indicate runners in blinkers that are reverting to their optimum distances, having previously raced over unsuitably short or long ones. You should make a note of such contestants, as well as those whose concentration is also likely to be increased because, for the first time, they are due to be partnered by crack apprentices or top-flight jockeys. The reduction of the field of view, through being distracted when making its final run, may well allow the past losses a runner has caused to be recouped. Indeed, I have frequently not only increased my bank balance but also my conviction that far too many backers understandably, but often rather too dismissively, regard blinkers as the unmistakeable badge of the rogue racehorse!

You need to realise that the 'blinds', which substantially reduce the field of view available to a runner, can cause far greater concentration on the part of the horse and help to avoid the use of the whip which, as John Hislop has pointed out, it may well resent and demonstrate this fact by 'swerving, hanging away from the whip or even refusing the race altogether'. On this subject the following amusing tale about the late Eph Smith is worth recalling. On one occasion Eph was riding Royal Charger, a two-year-old, for Sir Jack Jarvis. The colt was equipped with blinkers for the first time but Jack ordered his jockey on no account to hit him. In the event, Eph was beaten by a head when the slightest tap might have won the race. Jack was livid. 'I know I told you not to hit him,' he shouted, 'you could have at least waved it at him.' Eph shouted back, 'what the bloody hell's the good of waving it at a horse in blinkers; he can't bloody see it!'

STRATEGY 18:

Racing by Ear

Many true stories could be related about fortunes won on the strength of information, while much-needed sums, rather than windfalls, have been wrested from bookmakers; such was certainly the case when trainer Ron Thompson (who does not fling his money about) made a fraternal gesture to local striking miners at Stainforth, by tipping them Kindred, the winner of The Grey Horse Selling Hurdle at nearby Sedgefield, during the miners' dispute. One man who knows all about the worth of what in betting circles is known as *the word* is Ladbrokes' bookmaking supremo, Ron Pollard, and, significantly, he is sceptical about the value of possible information from owners and trainers. In fact, his advice, if you want to lose money, is to go and stand in Ladbrokes' main credit office and back all the horses that are backed by owners and trainers.

Having often written of the 'blinkers of hope and optimism' that blind many connections, I share some of Pollard's scepticism. However, I am mindful that the tips that jockey Marcus Armytage has given *Daily Telegraph* readers as the tipster 'Whistler' are often well in profit and have thus disproved the centuries old adage about jockeys being the world's worst tipsters!

Perhaps the most productive way of becoming party to the 'darkest secrets' of training establishments (some of which years ago once led the members of the massively successful 'Hermits of Salisbury Plain' syndicate to virtually imprison their stable staff) is to analyse the information from training quarters given (most comprehensively) in the *Daily Mirror,* the *Daily Mail,* the *Daily Express,* or the *Sporting Life* and *Racing Post.* Even *The Times* features news from Newmarket stables (the quality of which once allowed Jeffrey Barnard, one of the most entertaining of present-day racing scribes, to cope with a bankruptcy order from the Inland Revenue for £598.84). Typically, Jeffrey immediately placed a Yankee bet on four horses running at an evening meeting at Pontefract that the Newmarket correspondent of 'The Thunderer' had tipped. After a couple of drinks, Barnard retired to bed, only to discover that all four of his horses had won, so making him £2,235 the richer!

What I suggest is that detailed analysis be made of the fates of those horses 'touted' by gallops watchers employed by one or more of the above newspapers. In this way, much of the useless 'chaff' can be winnowed away and the information you are left with may then allow the backer to put some 'wheat in the bin'. Sadly, most so-called 'inside information' would be better kept under wraps, as is indicated by the dire fates of horses whose contracting prices in the betting market often reflect misplaced confidence in their chances.

STRATEGY 19:

Applying a Little Psychology

In *The Encyclopaedia of Gambling,* a weighty tome, Peter Arnold makes the vital point that you can obtain in excess of the 'true odds' against a horse's chance of winning by 'applying a little psychology'. What Arnold's cunning approach actually involves is deciding which runners, rated as having good chances on form, are likely as a result of having either a far from famous handler or being entrusted to an unfashionable jockey to be passed over by so many punters that bookmakers are likely to extend their odds. Arnold even argues that the off-putting names of some horses such as Mark's Methane, for example, means that many punters steer well clear of them. This guarantees that they 'go off' at really good odds!

I am not absolutely sure about this since the humble request of many of my acquaintances for the mere name of a winner persuades me that, even if I wrote down something that called their parentage into doubt, they'd write it down on a betting slip! However, Arnold's further point about the xenophobia and jingoistic patriotism on the part of we British often guarantees that classy French or Irish raiders line up for (or even win) English races at generous odds which belie their actual chances on form. Take, for example, a recent Boxing Day, when the prestigious King George VI Chase was run at Kempton. Here a Bonne Noël was certainly enjoyed by the connections of Nupsala since prejudice against French chasers in general conspired with sentimentally inspired over-confidence in Desert Orchid to guarantee a Gallic victory at gargantuan odds. As Nupsala's trainer later commented, he could hardly believe the prices on offer at Kempton and when Algan won the 'King George' for him at 10–1 in 1995 he had the same reaction.

Irish trainers too, while enjoying well publicised successes at Cheltenham's March Festival, occasionally slip in a winning runner at a less prestigious English or Scottish venue. Indeed, within a space of under ten days, Irish trainers Michael Kauntze, J. S. Bolger and M. McDonagh sent over three horses to run at Kempton, Doncaster and Chepstow respectively. All duly won at the value odds of 13–2, 5–1 and 7–2 which helped pay the costs of my impending racing holiday 'over the water'.

The fact that some little-known names have featured in the lists of riders with the highest 'winners-to-runners' ratios confirms the wisdom of not discounting horses that are unfashionably ridden. Some apprentices too are, to say the very least, unlikely to lessen the prospects of their mounts. Moreover, if you study the statistics relating to the number of occasions that handlers send out horses that are placed, as opposed to winning, many smaller ones turn out to be more successful than punters tend to think.

Sadly too, such is the depth of sexist prejudice against lady jockeys that their mounts often start at over-generous odds that do not accurately reflect their chances. Admittedly, Gee Armytage disproved this potentially lucrative belief, but this was in a most untypical race – the Grand National – and she was, after all, riding a horse, Gee A, that sounded as if it was her namesake. However, in other races in which lady jockeys have competed, nothing – not even the popularity of the Princess Royal – has reduced the odds of the horses they have ridden. Instead, many victories involving the fairer sex (even Royal ones at Redcar, Towcester and Ascot, on Gulfland, Cnoc Na Cuille and Ten No Trumps) have concerned outsiders in the betting. Indeed, I am sure that almost invariably when a racehorse is partnered by a lady rider who is due to take on male rivals the odds against its chances are inflated by bookmakers to a degree which reflects their chauvinism, rather than their commonsense.

The truth is, of course (as everyone knows who has compared the times taken by winners of ladies' races at point-to-point meetings with those taken by winners ridden by men), that if you back a lady jockey you can be sure that she will be doing her utmost to strike a blow for her sex, by confounding the belief that its members lack the strength or skill to ride their male rivals into the ground.

This point was certainly borne out by Katie Rimell who in true Corinthian style left her fellow jockey, former SAS officer, Broderick Munro-Wilson, well behind, along with many other males in the Horse and Hound steeplechase run at Stratford-upon-Avon. After dismounting from Three Counties, Katie was greeted by what Brian Beel of *The Times* described as 'whoops of joy' and received 'unstinting praise' from racegoers for riding out her grandmother's game hunter so vigorously that, just before the line, in a thrilling finish she was able to pip Bajan Sunshine, ridden by crack amateur Charlie Farrell. However, despite her cool display of power and expertise in the saddle, Katie was patronised by *Sporting Life's* correspondent Steve Taylor who, with incredible condescension, could only comment that – 'as she gains experience Miss Rimell will be of more assistance to her mount!' As it happened, Katie had steered it to its second successive

'Horse and Hound' victory. In contrast to Taylor, I tend to look with favour on the only jockeys whose 'conformation' can prove as pleasing to my eye as that of their mounts, and whose true grit, panache and gutsy determination to win can be virtually guaranteed.

STRATEGY 20:

Profiling Winners

Profiling has become a highly effective part of police work since its indications of the likely characteristics of those responsible for particular crimes can expedite their arrest. Interestingly, now that data on the many previous winnings of many races is printed in such weekly newspapers as the *Sporting Life Weekender* and also appears in Peter Braddock's book *Big Race Winners,* it is possible for 'profiles' to be drawn up of possible equine heroes, as opposed to human villains. Most usefully, the *Weekender* provides statistics for all flat and jumps races run on Fridays and Saturdays and these indicate the average odds and weights of the horses that have won these events during the preceding decade. The consequences of having placed a level pound on the ten favourites and ten second favourites in these races are also revealed, as is the average number of days the winners of these races had been away from the racecourse and the percentage of winners that had been previously placed first, second or third.

The very first time I aimed to disprove Henry Ford's assertion that 'history is bunk', I had a truly golden time at a Hereford jumping meeting. In the first race on the particular Saturday card I scrutinised, the *Weekender's* records led me to look for a 13–1 chance in the betting forecast. Another indication that a four-year-old should be my choice led me to Tockander and Willeson. As it happened, the former failed to go to post and the latter duly won at 7–1! In the next race Karene qualified on the strength of his 4–1 quote and four years, but failed to beat Big Aitch, the red hot 4–9 favourite. In the third race that I profiled, Thar an Bharr (quoted in the betting forecast at the indicated odds of 9–1), came as close to the magic age of 7.7 years as anything else in the field. He did not start at this enticing rate owing to the withdrawal of a better fancied runner, but I was quite happy when he trotted up by 15 lengths at 5–2.

Thar an Barr's jockey, Richard Dunwoody, duly booted home another winner that I had again selected according to this 'historical precedence' method of horse race selection. This, Tailored to Taste, carried 10st 8lb – exactly the average of the weights carried by the previous ten winners of the Russ Watkin's Handicap Chase! Incredibly, as 'the rag' in this four runner contest, he was allowed to go off at 20–1, before prevailing by a neck in a thrilling finish. The method's next indication for a novice hurdle – Major Match – was unplaced, but Glenweaving's success at 15–2 in the last race on this memorable Hereford card meant that, on its first 'trial' day, the 'precedence' method produced a 35 points profit on level stake betting.

Clearly, as far as horse racing goes, there are lessons in the past whose applications to the future can prove most profitable. This belief certainly inspires Craig Thake of the *Racing Post* to produce his '10 Year Trends' feature to cover major races. The following represented his view of the late season Zetland Stakes which, most encouragingly, happened to concur with my own, which, it may be recalled, was presented earlier in this book when Strategy 4 was discussed.

2.10: Asko Appliances Zetland Stks (1m2f)

	WINNER	AGE	WEIGHT	SP	TRAINER	BEST RUN
94	1 **Double Eclipse**	2	8-09	4-1JF	M Johnston	won Pontefract maiden (1m2f)
93	1 **Double Trigger**	2	8-09	3-1^{2}F	M Johnston	won Redcar maiden (1m1f)
92	041 **Bob's Return**	2	8-12	14-1	M Tompkins	won Pontefract maiden (1m)
91	31 **Bonny Scot**	2	8-12	2-1F	L Cumani	won Haydock maiden (1m)
90	222231 **Matahif**	2	8-12	4-1	R Armstrong	won Nottingham maiden (1m2f)
89	01 **Rock Hopper**	2	8-12	13-2	M Stoute	won Nottingham maiden (1m2f)
88	10 **Mamaluna**	2	8-07	9-1	G Harwood	won Chepstow maiden (1m)
87	21 **Upper Strata**	2	8-07	15-8F	L Cumani	won Wolverhampton maiden (1m1f)
86	01 **Grand Tour**	2	8-11	10-1	W H-Bass	won Hamilton maiden (1m)
85	121 **Highland Chieftain**	2	9-04	13-8F	J Dunlop	won Newmarket nursery (1m)

FAVS: +**£0.16**; 2ND FAVS: -£4.33

'The Asko Appliances Zetland Stakes (Listed) (2.10) at Newmarket also features a hat-trick bid, in this case from Mark Johnston. His last two winners of this event were once-raced winning maidens and his runner today, Polar Eclipse, obviously fits the bill.'

As Thake's 'history lesson' suggested would be the case, Double Eclipse enhanced Johnston's impressive training record in the 'Zetland' and, in doing so, confirmed the wisdom behind another two strategies in this book – ie. number 1, as well as number 4. Not for nothing, it would seem, was a system once called the 'converging factors' plan!

The Asko Appliances Zetland Stakes (Listed) (2.10) at Newmarket also features a hat-trick bid, in this case from Mark Johnston.

His last two winners of this event were once-raced winning maidens and his runner today, Polar Eclipse, obviously fits the bill.

STRATEGY 21:

Buying Money in Sellers

K. Morgan is often associated with several successful gambles on early season types! The day after I had read these words in a magazine, I was at Stratford races with a friend who told me he had just seen £400 staked on Morgan's Super Sol at 4–1. Within minutes this well-informed racegoer collected £2,000 in cash on this enterprisingly ridden winner of a selling hurdle! Understandably then, many imagine a selling race is often the medium of a successful gamble. Such a 'turn up', whether justifiably or not, can create a suspicion in some minds that most sellers are rigged. I do not have such an exaggerated view, but would rather suggest that research into the behaviour of selling race specialists may pay good dividends.

There are, of course, other reasons connected with the runners, rather than the handlers, involved in sellers that lead many backers to ignore these particular races. The main one is that they only attract horses of the lowest class. However, this can be profitably exploited. If the majority of selling race entrants are indeed such 'no hopers' then those who do not deserve this dismissive tag may well have outstanding claims since they face little serious competition.

I know that some would claim the horses which land gambles in sellers appear to have no form to recommend them prior to their victories, but, in fact, this conclusion is often belied if you take the trouble to delve back deeply into the form book. This point emerges from one of Brough Scott's contributions to a most entertaining anthology of his racing articles, *On and Off the Rails.* Brough tells how thorough form book scrutiny could have highlighted the prospects of Millfield Royal, a plater that once landed a gamble for Martin Pipe and his intrepid gambling friend, table tennis ace Chester Barnes. 'If only our early morning brains had put the old books in the car we could have read the form which made Barnes pick out Millfield Royal for Pipe at the Newmarket sales. For she had won both as a two-year-old and as a three-year-old and. . . once finished fifth in a better class race at Newcastle. The form was there!'

In my research into sellers, I have come across two separate indications that information regarding runners in handicap sellers which emanates from small gambling stables is often inspired. Many winners of selling races are returned at attractive odds because landing bets at them is virtually obligatory, given the conditions of these events which do much to supplement the incomes of racecourse executives. Commonly, winning platers are 'bought in' by their connections for three times the prize money they capture and thus the deficit has to be made up with winning wagers.

For this reason alone scrutiny of market moves for the runners of particular handlers and owners who are considered selling race specialists should provide some useful data with which to monitor the betting market and identify significant 'springers' or favourites within it. When analysing selling race form the following points are in my view worth considering.

1. Whether some horses are expensively 'bought in' by their connections. High outlays may well be 'recouped' by further gambles in sellers – sometimes even in non-selling events.

2. Whether a horse that has run disappointingly in sellers over a particular distance is tackling a different trip for the first time. It is a legitimate 'finesse' within racing for a trainer to run a horse over an unsuitable distance in order that its potential (when conditions are in its favour) cannot emerge.

3. Whether particular trainers send out 'dark horses', ie. those with no previous public form, to make winning debuts in sellers. Debutants, particularly from unfashionable yards, may have revealed to their handlers that they are much better than their modest purchase prices suggested or are a 'cut above' other first season platers. *Trainers' Review* will reveal whose first-time-out runners in sellers should be noted.

4. Whether a horse has been running in non-selling races and is being dropped down to plating class for the first time. If it is, this is well worth noting, as is the possibility that it may have previously run fast enough to be rated by a time expert. Not many platers receive speed ratings but, if they have come to a watchholder's attention, this may suggest they may 'run the legs off' their opponents, as might private handicap ratings that suggest they are well clear of their rivals on form.

5. Whether some runners in auction events carry weights (illogically determined by their purchase prices as yearlings) that would be far higher were they to be assessed on their past form as two-year-olds.

6. Whether horses are being sent long distances to run in sellers, particularly those carrying poor prize money. Given the price of petrol, it could be argued that such 'raiders', especially those from struggling yards, may well be gambled on successfully. To check on this factor *Horses in Training* and a good map will prove useful.

7. Whether a top-flight 'job' jockey or leading apprentice (whose ability hardly entitles him to the weight allowance he usually receives) has been engaged to ride, or replaces a less impressive-looking pilot previously listed. Similarly, if a jockey or apprentice has been released from his commitment to his retaining stable and is being allowed to take an 'outside' ride; this hint is worth considering.

8. Whether a springer's closing odds in the betting market have shortened by a greater percentage than the odds of other runners have shortened. A selling race favourite whose odds have been only marginally trimmed may, in fact, not be the 'best-backed' runner.

9. Whether a runner has been unsuccessfully gambled on in past sellers. If so, it may be out to retrieve previous heavy losses. If it is due to encounter different conditions (a shorter or long distance or a change of going or type of track) it may well 'atone'!

10. Whether the ages of the runners or the time of year when the seller is being run make the task of winner finding easier or more difficult. Plating form (as in non-selling races) often tends to work out better from May to mid-September, whereas, because platers are still developing in their second season and run over many varying distances, sellers confined to three-year-olds are often 'trappy' affairs that are difficult to assess. On the other hand, four-year-old platers tend to run rather more consistently.

11. Whether, by virtue of having won a valuable seller at a top-class track, a horse seems to face an easier task in a plate to be staged at a less prestigious meeting and which carries far less prize money.

12. Whether the presence of runners from particular yards in sellers at particular meetings at certain times of year augurs well for their chances.

13. Whether a runner has taken part in a 'key race' of which the form has worked out particularly well.

The following is a list of trainers whose runners in sellers (that attract market support) are in my view worth considering:

C. Allen
A. Bailey
R. Bastiman
M. Bell
J. Berry
M. Blanshard
N. Callaghan
P. Calver
M. Camacho
W. Carter

C. Cyzer
S. Dow
M. W. Easterby
D. Elsworth
P. Fielden
R. Hodges
W. Jarvis
P. Makin
A. Moore
B. Morgan
M. Naughton
W. O'Gorman
M. Prescott
Mrs. J. Ramsden
Mrs. M. Reveley
M. Ryan
B. Stevens
C. Thornton
W. Turner
M. Usher
J. Wharton
J. White
D. Wilson
Capt. J. Wilson

STRATEGY 22:

Following the Hunters

I once read an article penned by a tipster who claimed to be very well-qualified academically and hence worth heeding. His main contention was that one type of race was, perhaps rather surprisingly, worthy of specialisation. If I was forced to make a similar claim then I would opt for the hunter chase. My reasoning is that it is invariably far less competitive than any other event staged 'under rules' – only slightly less so perhaps that its junior relation, the point-to-point contest.

The hunter chase season starts at the beginning of February, thus offering some opportunity to defray the heavy expenses of Christmas and January. It closes at the end of May, with the final 'Horse and Hound' Hunters' Championship run at my local course, Stratford-upon-Avon. This highly competitive race, which usually involves a thrillingly close finish and some of the loudest cheering heard at Stratford all season, thanks to a bumper crowd of truly sporting spectators, is rather untypical of the majority of 'run of the mill' hunter chases. In these for most of the season there are many 'stand out' bets since frequently large numbers of 'no-hopers' take on a mere handful of horses which have a genuine chance and the latter can be easily identified by those punters who take the trouble to use specialist hunter form services or buy guide books. Some have subscribed to the *Hunterchase Ratings* form service, MacKenzie and Selby's *Hunterchasers and Point-to-Pointers* (referred to as the enthusiasts' bible), and supplement their study with the *Sporting Life's* weekly point-to-point results service. In addition, perhaps they may buy *The Pointer* from racecourse vendors which provides ratings and comments for runners in hunter chases as well as those taking part in chases and hurdles under NH rules.

Another useful service, available on subscription to the hunter chase fan, is the *Point-to-Point Index,* which provides the backer with an up-to-date merit rating of every horse with assessable form shown in a point-to-point or hunter chase. By late April, the Index lists well over 3,000 horses in alphabetical order. This weekly booklet is in my view a 'must' if you like to make your own decisions by looking at past form and will also help you with background on a horse's ability. The ratings should enable you to quickly sort out the 'wheat' from the 'chaff'. Indeed, within a few minutes of the runners being announced, many can be eliminated on account of their low ratings and you can scrutinise the form of the remainder before the betting market has had time to form.

Then, of course, when it comes to betting, the user of the Index is at a distinct advantage since, within seconds of a market move for any horse, you can have access to its previous form. Brian Beel, who produces the Index and *Hunterchase Ratings,* like MacKenzie and Selby, is a leading authority on hunterchasers and, in an article once published in an edition of the now defunct *Winning Ways* racing annual, produced a masterful guide to obtaining betting value. He describes the adjustments that need to be made to ratings given to hunterchasers to take account of the going, the course and distance they are due to race over, and the jockeys who have been engaged to ride them. Understandably, he feels that distance and jockeyship represent the most crucial factors which can influence the performances of hunterchasers. Apart from so many gilt-edged money making opportunities, hunter chases (especially via the exploits of those now emulating such game Corinthians as Caroline Beasley, who captured both the Cheltenham and Aintree Foxhunters' Chases), can I believe provide a truly sporting, as well as exciting, spectacle.

So, I can heartily recommend you consider hunterchasers. If racegoers find they have left their copies of MacKenzie and Selby behind, they could do worse than stand next to a racegoer who has taken the trouble to paste the recent form of the runners into an exercise book and try a little 'earwigging' and eavesdrop on his tip. Sadly, the last time I tried this, I was on a good thing that fell when well in contention on the final circuit!

PART FOUR: WINNING WAYS IN RACEHORSES

STRATEGY 23:

Potential for Improvement

As you may well have gathered by this stage in the book, I have a fondness for analysing form ratings as this may allow inferences to be drawn about possible improvements by some racehorses next time out. Ratings such as those provided by Howard Parker in the *Sporting Life* are sufficiently comprehensive to show if a horse, on the basis of a high form rating for the previous season, has a chance of defeating its rivals. Sometimes, a runner's disappointing form and lower form rating for the current season can be belied if it encounters track conditions (going, distance and topography) that correspond with those over which it has previously prevailed. Some animals improve dramatically when, for the first time, they are ridden by crack apprentices or really gifted top-flight jockeys. Many astute judges of the latter, among them Noel Murless, had a high regard for the Brazilian Braulio Baeza and his enterprising ride on Roberto when this colt defeated the previously unbeaten Brigadier Gerard in the Benson and Hedges Gold Cup at York in 1972.

Skilful reading of the races you see on the course, watching 'live' on television, or replaying on a video recorder, may provide hints that some contestants could show improved form next time out. Moreover, careful scrutiny of the form book may reveal the presence of propitious looking comments such as 'significant late headway' or 'nearest finish' by the names of certain runners. I have also noticed that in some of *Timeform's* advertising particular emphasis is placed on the appearance of a large 'P' alongside a few of the ratings provided by this, Britain's best known form service. This particular symbol denotes that there is 'a very strong presumption that the horse in question is capable of form much better than he has so far displayed.' Interestingly, as in *Timeform*, the letter 'P' occasionally appears against some other form ratings – those of Howard Parker of the *Sporting Life*.

Lightly raced horses, or rested ones that are described in specialist form books as likely to 'run well when fresh', may show improved form against jaded rivals. Significantly, Ryan Price always claimed that it took a fresh horse (like his own Soldier Rose) to win the gruelling 2¼ mile late-season marathon, The Cesarewitch. Some analysts feel that, in winning or being placed, horses which belie their lowly form ratings or long odds in the betting (thus exceeding the expectations of form experts and possibly the estimations of their 'connections') may run even more impressively next time out. Others believe that victory in fast time by a considerable margin, especially if this represents a large proportion of short race distances (5 or 6 furlongs on the flat or 16 'over the sticks') augurs extremely well for a horse's prospects in its next race.

A change of activity can also prove therapeutic and allow a horse to display considerable improvement when it reverts to its customary task. National winner Corbiere's improved form after being hunted has been well documented and during a recent National Hunt season, after making a fool of his trainer, David

Hodgson, in hurdle races, Adare went and won a chase at massive odds. Ill luck in past running experienced by horses that have dwelt at the start or have been badly hampered, baulked or forced to race alone may have prevented them from winning their races and these contestants may run far better next time out. Injudicious riding, such as that which some feel Greville Starkey was guilty of on Dancing Brave in the 1986 Derby may, if unrepeated, allow a horse to show it can run much more impressively on its next outing. For example, in the case of Dancing Brave, Pat Eddery steered him to a convincing revenge victory over his Derby conqueror in the King George VI Stakes at Ascot.

When I am tempted to draw conclusions that some horses may well improve on their previous form next time out, I remind myself of the need to base this hope on relevant and comprehensive statistics. Amongst ready made examples of these, some that I have found extremely useful are presented in a *Sporting Life* feature called *Ahead of the Handicapper*. This not only shows the official Jockey Club handicap rating a declared runner raced off in its last three outings in handicap company, but, even more usefully (if one wants to decide if a handicapper is an improving type), shows its 'current' official rating from which it is due to race and, crucially, that from which it will do so if it runs in coming handicaps.

The five handicap ratings provided for easy reference are immensely useful because they show if a horse has raced consistently well, has been erratic, is off form or, far more significantly, has improved steadily to reach its latest handicap mark or, in reaching it, seems to have left its hitherto undistinguished form well behind it. By 'charting' the many movements up and down the official Jockey Club ratings of the runners due to contest handicaps on any racing day, and also by indicating those which have had the advantage of a run after the date on which their most recent 'impending' handicap ratings were compiled, the expert responsible for this most thoroughly researched *Sporting Life* feature has greatly simplified the task of those who like to have improving horses on their side.

I am one of these and, as such, once looked to novice hurdler Samfen to pay my Christmas expenses. On the day after Boxing Day, this horse's new 'impending' rating of 29 was over double his current one of 13, from which he was due to contest a novices handicap at Wetherby. Moreover, the detailed data also supplied in this impressive *Sporting Life* feature showed that, crucially, Samfen had run after the date on which his 'new' handicap rating of 29 had been compiled. The fact that Samfen's only potential rival (according to the set of five handicap ratings), The Lodge Prince, had not had an outing since his own 'new' handicap rating had been compiled, made me even more confident that Samfen would prevail, especially since he was due to race at Wetherby – a far less prestigious National Hunt track than Ayr where he had previously raced. In the event Samfen won easily at 9–2!

The *Sporting Life* also publishes a weekly list showing the very latest changes in the official ratings of all handicappers that are good enough for Jockey Club officials to assess. So incidentally does its rival the *Racing Post*.

Three developments over the sticks provided me with useful reminders of the extent to which, when winning their races, some horses improve considerably on their past running. Perhaps many do this to the greatest extent after their first run of the season. Indeed, this view led Josh Gifford to be highly indignant when the Fontwell stewards, some time ago, asked him to explain the improvement shown by winning 3–1 favourite Musical Mystery, compared with his seasonal debut at vastly dissimilar Wincanton where he was beaten about half a furlong. 'Surely the stewards expect improvement on a horse's first run' was Gifford's understandable reaction.

However, were stewards not to enquire into vastly improved form, they would be criticised and, when they do not ask questions, there is sometimes someone who will protest vehemently. This was once the case when Barney Curley (whose spectacular Irish coups caused the Jockey Club to delay granting him a licence to train in Britain) objected that the Sandown stewards had failed to ask any questions when Robin Goodfellow trounced a horse that had previously beaten him by eight lengths.

Sometimes, the post-race comments of the 'connections' of winners that leave their previously disappointing form well behind them can provide clues to ways of inferring that other runners may be about to similarly distinguish themselves. For example, in once commenting that the fitting of blinkers to his Broken Wing had allowed this young hurdler to leave his previous 'goatish' form well behind him, Nicky Henderson confirmed the fact that the initial wearing of this particular aid to concentration can allow some horses to improve on their past form by as much as two stones. Significantly, Broken Wing had been a well-backed but unsuccessful favourite on his previous run without 'the shades' at Stratford.

Racehorses, of course, may eventually improve sufficiently to 'bring home the bacon' for many other reasons. For example, they may be about to re-encounter distances, going, conditions or terrain on particular courses that have previously allowed them to triumph. Horses tackling their optimum trips after having raced over shorter or longer ones or mudlarks (like Teenoso in the 1983 Derby) or firm ground specialists, who experience the extremes of going they relish, will often revert to winning form. Many shrewd judges – for example, the compilers of the excellent *Superform* annuals – also believe that the opportunity to race on particular tracks can, in the case of recently disappointing types, rekindle their enthusiasm for racing, or even restore a zest for this activity in those perhaps unfairly dismissed as 'dogs'. *Superform's* expert racereaders feel that on the flat such 'miracle cures' often seem to take place on tracks such as Chester, Epsom or Brighton whose tight turns may allow jockeys to 'kid' horses that perform less generously elsewhere.

Incidentally, an interesting point made in the introduction to all *Superform* annual form books that 'more horses go back than improve', and another equally telling comment, by trainer Clive Brittain, that 'not many horses are really genuine' suggests that, if the backer can find a reliable horse that appears to be on the upgrade, he may well be on to something. There are two ways of determining whether a horse is dropping in class and thus may be about to improve on its previous form. The first involves dividing the number of a runner's previous victories into its total earnings and comparing the resultant figure with the prize money for which it is about to compete. If the former figure exceeds the latter by a good deal, a horse could be said to be 'dropping in class'. The second is if you see a horse about to run for less prize money than previously at a less prestigious meeting than that it last raced over.

STRATEGY 24:

Race Fitness

Apart from the fact that some trainers are adept at producing horses that can win first time out, even after lay-offs as long as several years in some impressive cases, there is no doubt that horses fit from having had a recent run often enjoy a distinct advantage. Indeed, I have noted the significant fact that the *Racing Post* lists horses successful in the past seven racing days. The problem, however, is how to gauge the likely extent of the advantage conferred by a recent 'pipe opening' placed or winning run – a factor that the author of *Braddock's Complete Guide to Horse Race Selection and Betting* considers so crucial he makes it the virtual cornerstone of his selection procedures.

The solution to this problem was suggested to me by the impressively frequent and sequential wins of the sprinter Chaplin's Club who, in under a fortnight, added greatly to his trainer's tally of wins! Having talked to sprinters and some marathon runners I now feel there are sound physiological reasons why recent participation in a race is likely to confer a greater advantage on those asked to run over a short distance rather than a long one. Obviously, unless a sprint (as for infant schoolchildren or two-year-old racehorses, given their immaturity) is something of a 'distance race in disguise', it should not take as much out of those participating in it, as is usually the case with those involved in a far more gruelling and taxing slog over a long distance, of which, of course, the Grand National is a well-known extreme example.

Given that steeplechasers and long-distance performers on the flat need time to recover from their protracted and hence, ultimately, more taxing exertions, I suggest that (discounting two-year-old races) you concentrate your attention on mature sprinters that turn out after a recent run. Like human athletes, equine sprinters (of which Chaplin's Club was a fine example), 'peak' for a short period in a season and within this spell can often register victory after victory. If mature sprinters not only have the benefit of a recent promising run, but are well drawn and top-rated by a time expert, they may well turn out to be true 'pigeon catchers'. Over the sticks, the statistics also show that in two-mile hurdle races, rather than much more exhausting steeplechases, runners with recent promising form are frequently successful!

Remembering that, as with any method of racehorse selection, theory is all very well, I recently put the 'fitness plan' to the test. I did so at the beginning of the season when a major advantage is enjoyed by contestants that are 'wound up'. What I found on my random test day was that, with two-year-olds discounted, of six sprinters top-rated by the *Daily Mail's* private handicapper Formcast, that had also been placed first, second or third within 28 days or less, three won (at 7–1, 7–2 and 11–4), one was second at 5–4, another was third at 3–1 and only one was unplaced. Clearly, one day's races cannot prove a conclusive test but it does in my view mean this strategy is worth considering in your search for winners.

STRATEGY 25:

Relative Maturity

All parents will appreciate that when children first go to school some have a 'head start' over others, simply because they are so much older than their so-called 'contemporaries'. Some infant school children can, in fact, be almost 12 months older than their classmates, at a time when this age differential represents a crucially large proportion of the total time they have had in which to grow and mature. Significantly, even the old-fashioned, but still surviving, 11-plus examination makes some allowance for the fact that some candidates, like my own daughter, for example, are penalised by being far younger than some of their rivals.

A method I have christened the 'school gate' plan seeks to capitalise on the fact that many of the youngest racehorses of all – two-year-olds – are, in fact, well over this minimum age. Many readers will be aware that, irrespective of the actual dates on which they were foaled, all thoroughbreds are given an official birthday of January 1st. Crucially this means that when the flat racing season starts in March, some debutants may be as old as two years and two months, through having been foaled in January two years previously, while others with birthdays at the end of June may not, in fact, be two-year-olds at all, but rather immature animals that have only had just over 18 months in which to grow, develop and mature.

Fascinatingly, a recent season-long survey of two-year-olds showed that those with January foaling dates registered almost double the number of wins than those achieved by first season runners born in June. Astonishingly, the statistics almost totally vindicated the thinking I first engaged in, when noticing how large were some of my daughter's infant school chums. *Winners to Runners* percentages by foaling dates for two-year-olds, covering a recent whole season, read as follows:

January foaling	12.3%
February foaling	9.4%
March foaling	9.6%
April foaling	8.3%
May foaling	7.7%
June foaling	6.9%

Clearly these figures provide an almost complete statistical vindication of the wisdom of having age and experience on your side.

All in all, foaling dates can provide a useful key to the enigma that unknown and later, under-exposed, two-year-olds present. Interestingly, another 'key' to unlocking the prospects of such performers can be found if information on the average distances of races won by their sires' progeny is consulted. Such data can be found in the *Statistical Record*. One early season plan for you to consider is to allow two-year-olds points for their maturity – say twelve for a January foaling, ten for a February one, eight for March and so on, down to two for June. Then you add these to further points expressive of the relationship between average winning distances of sires' progeny and the distance of the race in question.

For example, a two-year-old in a five furlong sprint, sired by Fleet Allied (USA) would get twelve points for having a winning distance figure of 5.0, while one sired by Amboise, with a distance figure three times this at 15.00, would receive none!

12 pts for race distances shown as 5.0 – 6.0 furlongs
10 pts for race distances shown as 6.1 – 7.0 furlongs
8 pts for race distances shown as 7.1 – 8.0 furlongs
6 pts for race distances shown as 8.1 – 9.0 furlongs
4 pts for race distances shown as 9.1 – 10.0 furlongs
2 pts for race distances shown as 10.1 – 11.0 furlongs
0 pts for race distances shown as 11.00 furlongs or more

On the basis of points given for maturity and optimum race distance, a January foaled two-year-old by Fleet Allied, with his or her 24 pts, could be expected to go really well in an early season five furlong sprint.

STRATEGY 26:

Pace and Speed

As was once revealed in a fascinating *Arena* documentary on the contemporary English thoroughbred, this largely owes its speed to Arab bloodstock brought into this country several centuries ago. Interestingly, this programme also highlighted Ajdal, the veritable flying machine and July Cup winner whose fleetness of foot actually worried his trainer, Michael Stoute, after his charge had won the Dewhurst and had become a live 2,000 Guineas prospect. 'With all his speed I was worried he might not get the extra furlong' was Stoute's comment, made with hindsight after Ajdal had not only flopped over the testing Newmarket mile in the Guineas, but also had run just as disappointingly in the Derby.

As Brough Scott later most perceptively pointed out, 'speed is one thing, but how far will it stretch!' One who correctly answered that question in connection with Ajdal was Stoute's work rider, Tony Kimberley, who, after dismounting from a lead horse that Ajdal had trounced in a four furlong pre-Derby pipe-opener, prophetically, if ungrammatically, pronounced: 'That's not going to win no Derby. That'll win the July Cup!'

That victory does not always go to the swift is suggested by the fact that expert watchholders do not win the Tipsters' Nap Championship every time it is contested. However, Alex Bird, Britain's most successful professional punter since the war, and horse racing's best known guru, Phil Bull, have both set profitable store by time ratings whose positive indications are corroborated by encouragement from the form book. Indeed, the brand name of *Timeform* chosen by Bull for the most comprehensive and most highly respected set of racehorse assessment services should serve as a constant reminder to backers of how important it is to keep time on their side.

According to Dave Edwards (Stopwatch of the *Sporting Life*), this timely reminder is clearly needed as, in his view, time is 'arguably the most consistently ignored aspect of British racing'. This comment doubtless applies to the majority of backers and not to some of the best brains in racing, such as those of Bull and company. Indeed, the analysis and interpretation of race times has exercised Bull's mind so effectively that his *Timeform* organisation regularly claims to top rate around 30% of all winners on the flat and over the jumps.

However, there are problems with approaches to winner-finding based on the clock which do much to constitute what Dave Edwards has called the 'colossal, but not impossible, task of comparing times from topographically different courses and over different distances that have been recorded on different going conditions'. I believe if you make allowances for the three factors I indicate on page 121 you can reduce the worst 'ravages' of adopting solely time-based approaches. Taken together, these pointers should produce far more profitable results than any 'blind' adherence to time.

1. Apart from being proven over the distance of its impending race, a highly rated horse on time should have earned its speed figure on a topographically similar track and in a race of higher or at least equivalent class to that on which it is due to race.

2. The going which a time selection is about to encounter should be akin, or similar to, that prevailing when it impressed the watchholders.

3. Perhaps above all else, the 'time test' is a method of checking on and perhaps 'cracking' the form conundrum. It enables you not only to put a yardstick on horses, but also shows which races were 'falsely run' as well as which winners to suspect for having won shortish races in slow times.

Doubtless with such thoughts in mind, the proprietors of *Raceform's Handicap Book* publish the ratings of Split Second alongside the official Jockey Club handicap ratings. These alternative 'private handicap' ratings allow you well in advance of racing to take the measure of those horses shown to be well in on form and time. From this selection you can compile a short list of animals on which to do some further homework. As it happens, I am a great believer in the potential for profit implicit in any consensus of agreement between Howard Parker and Dave Edwards, since what these *Sporting Life* experts actually provide are two separate and complete 'private handicaps' based on form and time respectively.

PART FIVE: HINTS FOR HORSE WATCHERS

STRATEGY 27:

Racereading

The backer who is sufficiently wise and fortunate to visit a racecourse (one of the few places where, as John Welcombe once so feelingly put it, 'one can find people really enjoying themselves and glad to appreciate the gift of existence') is in an ideal position from which to adopt some potentially profitable on-course betting strategies. One of these is racereading, and now that video recordings of races are made not just by television viewers, but also sold by specialist concerns which cover the lowliest meetings, the penning of a few thoughts on this difficult art would seem appropriate.

Since a suggestion, made quite seriously, that each jockey should ride in the same distinctively different set of colours in every race is unlikely to appeal to the Owners' Association or to be adopted by the Jockey Club, prospective racereaders (especially since not even the *Racing Post* illustrates the colours associated with the runners in every race) would be wise to heed the advice that Jack Leach offers in his intriguingly named *Sods I have Cut on the Turf.* To Leach, former jockey, trainer and racing journalist, 'knowing the jockeys is the main thing in racereading'. Indeed, recognising the distinctive ways the leading 20 or so jockeys of his day sat on their mounts, as well as their idiosyncratic movements, give-away mannerisms and other revealing non-verbal behaviour, helped Leach not only to identify runners from the grandstand but, more importantly, to detect clues as to their immediate or future prospects.

The problem, however, with drawing conclusions from the riding of particular jockeys is that the very best of them provide very few hints of these prospects to their rivals or to those far more numerous 'riders in the stand'. Leach himself confessed that when he was riding he often made the mistake of thinking he'd got Steve Donoghue and Gordon Richards well beaten but they would keep 'pulling out a bit more'. Interestingly, and rather more recently, Bobby Elliott paid tribute to the similarly bewildering sight of Scobie Breasley on horseback. Elliott felt that the Australian maestro wanted a good deal of watching and admired him for not making it too obvious that he was having to ride a horse, for not revealing he was in trouble and for just sitting there 'niggling' and for not doing much more than that when he rode a finish!

In one memorable race – the 1964 Derby – Breasley so perturbed the connections of Santa Claus for coolly bringing home this 15–8 favourite to win by a short head, that he was never allowed to ride their champion colt again. Even more recently, another highly successful horseman and former trainer, Frankie Durr, applauded the sheer versatility of Lester Piggott that made this famous jockey so hard to assess when in the saddle. In 1981, Durr made the following comment: 'Piggott has no particular style of riding; he is a master of all styles. From the stands he creates all kinds of impressions and no impression. Ask a jockey who is riding next to him if Piggott is pushing his mount or just pretending and he won't be able to tell you!'

This is all very well, but how are prospective racereaders to make sense of what they see through their binoculars if some jockeys present such bewildering sights? Fortunately, this problem is a minor one as there are only one or two jockeys who are almost impossible to assess. Indeed, for much of the time a good deal can be learnt from observing the far more revealing riding of their many rivals.

Besides Jack Leach, another former jockey turned journalist, Bob Butchers (ex-Newsboy of the *Daily Mirror*) has passed on advice about the behaviour of jockeys to guide would-be racereaders. Interestingly, Butchers, in an article once written for the now defunct *Daily Mirror Punters' Guide,* indicated that this behaviour is often adopted to allow horses to run their races in particular styles that have been shown to suit them, or which it is believed will do so. He also makes the critical point that the pace at which a race is run may prevent a jockey from allowing his mount to adopt a suitable style of running.

Interestingly, Richard Baerlein believed that the rather moderate Derby field of 1986 did not allow Greville Starkey to capitalise on Dancing Brave's acknowledged speed, as this colt, 'basically took part in a three furlong sprint after a mile dawdle'. Sadly, when Starkey failed to win the Derby by about four feet or so, another point made by Butchers – that many 'grandstand critics make a scene when the horse they have backed seems to have left his effort too late' – was fully borne out. Whether or not Starkey came too late on Dancing Brave will be argued over for years, but what is undeniable is Butchers' further point that 'had many a losing jockey made his effort earlier he would not have finished so far up the field'.

At least Dancing Brave's Derby run provided a useful reminder to aspiring racereaders that the performance of a horse or a jockey should be seen from a perspective provided by a knowledge of what it requires in the way of optimum pace and running. Losing by a narrow margin should not be held against a horse or its jockey if it fails to encounter these, because they may constitute prerequisites for its success. In further commenting on racereading, Butchers has also made the important point that such prerequisites can vary greatly since some horses like to bowl along in front, to start off faster than others (like Dancing Brave over a mile and a half), or need to be held back in the early stages and then allowed to finish fast. There are also horses which have to be ridden at nearly the same pace throughout their races, those which have to be restrained, and others that, in contrast, have to be pushed along and kept up to their work.

Before watching a race, would-be racereaders who wish to profit from their observations are advised to take a leaf from top-flight jockeys who take the trouble to determine the particular paces and the ways in which races should be ridden to the advantage of the animals they are engaged to ride. Such information is readily available in such excellent guides as *Raceform Notebook, Racing Annuals* and *Superform* (which is published by the Furlong Press of Shoreham) and will allow what is eventually seen on the racecourse to be measured against a useful yard-stick.

When racereading there are, of course, several types of runners you can look out for, other than those who encounter pace or running they find ideal or unsuitable. Make a note, for example, of horses who have enough in reserve to lengthen their strides in the closing stages when their jockeys pick them up or give them a slight tap with their whips. Also jot down the names of the horses which run creditably without the encouraging competition of any nearby rivals, in other words those finishing well despite their isolation on one side of a track. Horses which have been baulked or knocked out of their strides, or have been denied a clear run or a fast break, or have run well from an unfavourable draw are also worth keeping any eye on, especially if they have taken part in sprints in which such ill-luck in running can prove critical.

You should also note any horses which, despite being hard held by their jockeys, still manage to win easily by several lengths. Similarly keep track of any runners finishing close up whose jockeys do not go for their whips or subject them to too much pressure. Such runners, as well as those running on after a finish in which they were unable to quicken because it concerned a distance that was too short for them can be spotted if racereaders avoid the understandable temptation to concentrate on the leading horses or on an animal in which they have a financial interest. Racereading with an eye to the future will be most successful if attention is paid to horses which, through failing to make the frame, run on to finish in fourth, fifth or sixth, or if the field is large, even further down. Many such finishers will suggest that they are likely to step up on these placings if, in future, they come under greater pressure from their jockeys.

Another key element in racereading is learning to recognise those contenders who should be disregarded in future. Such animals may have indicated that they were tired or in distress by hanging or rolling, as if drunk, off a straight course, or by switching their strides so that one moment they're leading with one foreleg and the next they put the other one down in front, or by swishing their tails. Significantly too, many horses which finish second are hard ridden and may not have recovered from their jockey's desperate urging by their next outings.

Perhaps the best advice that can be offered to prospective racereaders is to watch as many races and video recordings of these as possible. The latter allow endless opportunities for gaining experience and practice. In fact, readers with video recorders who wish to derive a good deal from watching races on their television screens are strongly advised, as a first step, to obtain a copy of *Riding to Win,* a Mirror Vision video tape, in which Willie Carson provides invaluable insight into the demanding role of successful racereading.

If you wish to extend your armchair scrutiny of this fascinating activity beyond the televised races you have personally recorded, then you can obtain recordings of Flat or National Hunt races from either Race-Tech of 85 Bushey Park, London or, rather more cheaply, from Pics on Day Video Sales Ltd, of 52A South Street, Worthing, Sussex. National Hunt enthusiasts who want to become more proficient racereaders are advised either to read *Born Lucky,* John Francome's entertainingly revealing autobiography, or to watch *Once in a Lifetime,* a video that features both the racereading and the perceptive comments of this consummate horseman.

Incidentally, readers without video recorders will find their reading of televised races, and those they watch on racecourses, will improve if they read *From Start to Finish,* John Hislop's manual for the novice jockey, available from some public libraries. It would be most gratifying if what I have written at least encourages some readers to try to solve what is perhaps the most difficult problem in racereading – recognising a horse that is running too freely and detecting one of its rivals that may well overhaul it and beat it to the line. As Jack Leach has put it, 'all too often, a horse that is leading in the closing stages is beaten by something that is in behind running lazily that will pull out far more at the finish'.

To anticipate such a development is not always easy and even experienced racereaders can fail to do so or make assumptions that are confounded at the death. The one 'rider in the stand' who invariably drew correct conclusions when it mattered was the 'head waiter' amongst jockeys, the late Harry Wragg. According to Leach, 'many a time when the crowd was shouting something home, Harry would quietly remark "there's one in behind that will win in a minute when the jockey lets it go".' He was invariably correct since the jockey on the horse he was watching would be seen to be the last to go for his whip or start 'scrubbing' along as a prelude to victory. Clearly, the prerequisite for successful racereading is the ability to remain undistracted.

STRATEGY 28:

Finding Winners by a Head

Those whose evaluations of good looks, well-being and personality I really envy, make up that minority of modern-day racegoers who can be described as shrewd 'paddock' judges. The advice they give and the selections they make are often 'inspired' and can prove very valuable – a fact confirmed by my recent analysis of the comments that *Timeform* most usefully makes on the conformation, looks and actions of racehorses. This revealed that certain descriptions of particular physical attributes often appear against the names of the horses that this famous form service rates most highly. Moreover, examination of the comments that *Raceform's* paddock judges present against the names of horses that win in any racing week, either on the flat or over jumps, will reveal that approximately a third of these were noted as 'looking well' before their victories.

In my sincere desire to be able to assess the potential of racehorses according to physical criteria, I have read countless guides to good conformation and well-being in racehorses and even, would you believe, gazed intently at my daughter's plastic 'Sindy' horse! My research has confirmed what I have long suspected; that assessing racehorses on their looks is a complex business and that to guide the beginner any conclusions resulting from this process should be presented under a few general headings – the first of which should be character. By this I do not mean eccentricity, singular mannerisms or idiosyncrasies, such as fondness for a pint of beer, but an individuality so physically apparent that it can seem the 'stamp of greatness' or at least of considerable superiority. Such a characteristic was certainly possessed by the champion sire Northern Dancer and just as strongly by his ancestor – The Tetrarch – a colt that, according to his jockey Steve Donoghue, had a personality that was enormous in that he 'commanded respect and attention whatever he did' and seemed to 'know everything there was to know about racing' even when he first set foot on a racecourse. Donoghue even went so far as to credit this striking-looking grey with a 'seventh sense'. Interestingly, his descendant, the champion sire Northern Dancer, showed something of this since he, and not his jockey, would decide precisely when he would sweep past his racecourse rivals.

Fortunately, like many human beings, racehorses can provide physical clues as to their possible possession of physical superiority, courage, boldness, cleverness, honesty, alertness, strength, powers of observation, concentration, intelligence, adaptability and obedience – attributes which, if present in good measure, perhaps help to provide what is often vaguely described as 'character'. Former jockey and trainer Jack Leach has claimed that if horses have 'presence', in that they carry themselves proudly and 'give the appearance of being able to lick creation', then they may have considerable potential – that is, of course, provided they are also sound and have good conformation.

A good deal of store is set by the belief that a horse's head is a very reliable index of character. Significantly, that noted judge John Hislop, when once commenting on the ideal physical attributes of an Epsom Derby winner, pointed out that 'such a champion rarely has a bad head – it may be small like Manna's or big like that of Windsor Lad, but it is never common or suggestive of a dishonest or cowardly disposition'. In Hislop's opinion, the first point to look for in the perfect Derby horse is a 'good head'. What this actually constitutes has been expressed through comparison with the head of a duchess or even of a fairy!

The purpose of such comparisons is to stress that a racehorse ought to carry its head 'regally'. Interestingly, King Edward VII's appropriately named Derby winner, Diamond Jubilee, possessed a head that was suitably suggestive of his independence, as well as his rather arrogant disdain for all save Herbert Jones, his splendidly clad jockey. Allegedly, Diamond Jubilee would allow no one else near him, not even his royal owner who, significantly, stood several steps away when posing for a photograph to commemorate this colt's Epsom triumph.

The imposing heads of Classic winners and other top-class racehorses are neat and well-formed, present a clear cut 'sculptured' appearance and feature broad flat foreheads. So if you are trying to pick the winner of prestigious races on the level, horses with heads reminiscent of those past champions that equine artists often manage to more effectively record for posterity than photographers should, perhaps, be given at least a passing glance.

Many judges believe that 'character' can be detected in the eyes of racehorses. Leach himself has revealed that he kept his eye open for the so-called 'look of an eagle' in the eyes of the yearlings he scrutinised. Perhaps such eyes – large, transparently clear, stolid, bright and gleaming with vitality and intelligence and set low and quite widely apart in the forehead – may provide a hint that a horse has something in his mind and temperament that will make him, if not a champion, at least a 'cut above' his rivals. It should, however, be pointed out that some experts scoff at the belief that a horse's eye is the window through which its 'magic spirit' or 'soul' can be seen. For example, in his article *Horse Faces,* Michael Schafer claims that 'a good deal of nonsense has been written about a horse's eyes'. Indeed, his advice to all those who gaze into these is not to 'humanise' their owners by seeing all the virtues (or lack of them) in these delicate organs. Such an anthropomorphism has led some to suspect the credentials of racehorses whose eyes are set close together – because this physiological peculiarity is something that many murderers apparently share.

Many judges believe that something of the character of a horse – that entity that does so much to determine how well it actually performs on the racecourse – may be revealed by its ears. Some feel that large to medium-sized, 'bold-looking', sensitive ears that point slightly inwards indicate a generous nature and that if these are cocked and alert, this may indicate that their owner thoroughly relishes having to race in public and has the even temper and extrovert character to make this activity one in which success is consistently achieved. Interestingly, if you study a picture of Spindrifter, the two-year-old that in 1980 won a record 13 races (ten of them in succession) it is clear that he has such 'alert' ears.

In contrast, floppy ears that are not pricked parallel to each other in a forward position, but held in one nearer the horizontal than the vertical, are believed to augur less well for their owner's chances. As for ear movement, if this features a constant 'flickering', this may be suggestive of moodiness or even of ill-temper, while a nervous, anxious disposition may be signalled by ears that move continually from side to side.

Many readers may well concur with the above comments and these may even help the casual racegoer make a profit, since a vital part of keeping ahead in the racing game involves trying to spot a winner on looks. However, my view is to proceed with extreme caution. The 'eyes' do not always have it, of course, but a mere glance at the comments in *Timeform* essays on the horses this form service rates the most highly does suggest that there is often a strong correlation between conformational splendour and excellence of racecourse achievement.

STRATEGY 29:

Studying Conformation

The difficulty of writing anything authoritative on the subject of conformation was once highlighted by the trainer Peter Walwyn. Writing in the *Daily Mirror Companion to Racing* in 1981, he recalled his response to a request that he write an article on the physical lines and shape of a horse. 'It's virtually impossible. It's rather like asking me to describe a pretty girl. One man can look at a horse and like it very much, but another may not be able to stand the sight of it. I may buy a horse that someone else considers a horrid thing and certainly I would never have bought some of the horses others buy, but many roads lead to Rome.' Despite such differences of expert opinion, which, in the view of 'Icarus' of the *Sporting Life*, make the study of conformation both 'fascinating and frustrating', it is possible to make some general observations on this subject that it should pay you to heed. Indeed, if you can tell whether your selection on non-physiological criteria, such as form and time, also appears to be a 'winner on looks', then so much the better!

Obviously, if a horse has good conformation – in other words if it is correctly built and balanced and its parts are in proportion to each other – then you are entitled to suppose that its training and previous racecourse performances will not have imposed undue strain on its 'framework' and that, when this carries its own body weight, as well as that of its jockey, it will not labour or become unbalanced under this payload. While, of course, perfect or excellent 'conformation' is no guarantee of success on the track (a fact confirmed each season by the lacklustre racing performances of so many expensive and handsome yearlings), its possession by a racehorse makes it more likely to win than would-be entrants for the equine equivalent of the Mr Punyverse contest.

Readers' visually registered perceptions of the physiological attributes of the unbeaten Bahram (seen on page 136) may be heightened still further if this colt has his physiological characteristics expressed in words. As for these, none could be more expressive than the following with which John Hislop paid tribute to the Aga Khan's second Derby winner. 'He has a beautiful head, masculine yet kind, the eye is full and round, the ears are a good size, yet delicately moulded and the face bloodlike and straight, neither convex or concave – his feet are truly made and uniform, his pasterns are of the right substance, length and slope and his fetlock joints are clean and strong. . . Bahram's cannon bones are just the right length, have substance in proportion to the general build of the horse and run perfectly into the knees, which are clean, well-formed and set at the correct angle in relation to the rest of the forelegs so that he is neither "back at the knee" (or like Brown Jack and many other stayers) "over at the knee". His shoulders are well-sloped and not heavy and his neck is of exactly the right length and development, the head perfectly set upon it. His withers are prominent but not too narrow, his girth is deep, there is ample freedom at the elbows, his ribs are well-sprung and he does not "run up" at the brisket. His

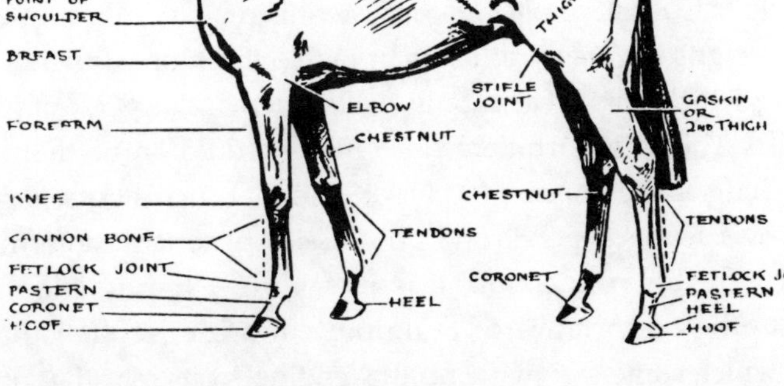
POLL
WITHERS
POINT OF HIP
LOINS
CROUP
ROOT OF DOCK
THROAT
SHOULDER
RIBS
FLANK
POINT OF BUTTOCK
POINT OF SHOULDER
THIGH
BREAST
STIFLE JOINT
ELBOW
GASKIN OR 2ND THIGH
FOREARM
CHESTNUT
KNEE
CHESTNUT
CANNON BONE
TENDONS
TENDONS
FETLOCK JOINT
CORONET
FETLOCK JOINT
PASTERN
PASTERN
CORONET
HEEL
HEEL
HOOF
HOOF

back is short, but he has great scope, since, apart from his well-sloped shoulders, his quarters are long. These are also strong, having the tail set at just the right point. The second thighs (gaskins) are particularly powerful and flow gradually out of the quarters. . . his hocks are strong and well made and his stifle is built to give freedom of action.'

As David Craig put it so succinctly in his *Penguin Guide to Horse Racing*, one of the most important factors in conformation (which might be simply described as the 'make and shape' of a racehorse) is the perpendicularity of the slope from the point of the shoulder to the point of the elbow. Besides an intelligent and handsome head, what is also desirable is a long, strong, light muscular neck (bringing the centre of gravity well forward), low free, well-placed elbows, sloping shoulders, high withers running well back, good depth at the brisket, body well ribbed up, a short back, powerful loins and quarters. . . broad gaskins, strong straight hocks, good fetlocks and pasterns and plenty of bone in the leg below the knee. The last named attribute (in a list that in many respects echoes many of Hislop's points about Bahram) is certainly something to look out for in jumpers.

When indicating which of these features to look out for in the paddock, Icarus of *Sporting Life* advised his readers to concentrate on spotting signs of *fitness* rather than tackle the more difficult task of deciding which horses seem built for the demanding task of jumping obstacles. This is unfortunate since many would argue that there is such a thing as the 'stamp of a chaser' and that such a horse's capacity to soar over fences depends on its possession of certain conformational features. In this connection, it is in my view impossible to over-estimate the importance of a jumper's hind legs, particularly its hocks, which some feel make up the 'engine' at its rear that provides it with the propulsion it needs to take off; indeed, if it is a Wayward Lad, a Desert Orchid or a Pendil, to positively 'spring' over a fence.

You should never forget that horses are not jumping animals by nature and that for them to be able to emulate those that are and to cushion the shock their suspension systems receive when they return to earth, they need to be strong, sound and supple, not only in their hind and forelegs, but also in their thighs, forearms, sloping shoulders, high withers and backs. The important point, that a jumper's hocks as well as being straight and wide (and certainly not 'sickle hocked' or 'cow hocked') should be under its centre of gravity, so as to give it good balance, provides a useful reminder that the best negotiators of obstacles are often rather balletic, Nijinsky-like performers whose stylish, artistic and fluent movements in take-off, flight and landing blind those who watch them to the strength on which they depend. Just as Nijinsky's power to soar gracefully through the air depended largely on his strength in the legs, so a horse's ability to soar over a fence depends on his ability to place his hocks far under his body and then use them to propel himself over this obstacle.

You can learn even more about conformation if other comments on particular conformational attributes are checked against photographs of horses that display these, such as appear in the highly collectable *Timeform Annual Guides to Racehorses.* Other collectable items, notably Players' and Ogden's cigarette cards showing past champions or Derby entrants for past seasons (such as 1929), if juxtaposed, will allow you to test your ability to spot a winner on looks. I looked all through those initially declared for the 1929 Derby, but must confess that 'Trigo' (whose appearance, like that of the 1913 winner 'Tagalie', did not flatter her) did not take my eye.

PART SIX: EXPLOITING THE BETTING MARKET

STRATEGY 30:

Cracking Tic-Tac

The fact that a group of key personnel on the racecourse have secrets so dark that they adopt a secret language with which to share them is confirmed by the energetic gesticulations of the tic-tacs who help to make the racecourse scene so much more colourful. Indeed their signs have done much to help promote ITV's betting guru John McCririck, who is one of racing's most colourful and unusual characters since Ras Prince Monululu. John McCririck only demonstrates a fraction of the signs that comprise the full repertoire of the tic-tacs. Fortunately, however, the special language of bookmakers, their secret codes and signalling methods can be 'cracked' and you can, with practice, become party to what for the majority of racegoers remains privileged information.

Bookmakers' communication systems largely involve special signs developed from Australian practices first used in the last century. They are given by tic-tacs whose expertise presents such a refreshing and colourful contrast to the use of ultra-modern electronic communication devices which, to a thankfully small extent, are now being seen on British racecourses. These particular bookmakers' agents fulfil a variety of functions. Some provide a 'trade' service that is absolutely vital – to transmit wagers that bookmakers need to make with colleagues on the course to cover their dangerously over-large liabilities on certain runners. These bets arrive at the course via direct telephone lines or the 'blower' as it is traditionally known. Indeed such covering money used to be 'blown' to the course by the Victoria Blower Company which acted for bookmakers who were lesser lights in their profession than leading layers like Ladbrokes. In practice, however, modern blower agents may not now find themselves receiving bets on telephones actually located in Tattersalls' ring. Even today the task of relaying these crucial wagers is often entrusted to a blower tic-tac who acts as a last living link in a chain of communications that stretches all the way, via another 'blower' agent, back to 'base' – a clearing house whose sole purpose is to enable over-committed office bookmakers to hedge their way out of danger. The tic-tacs who help to provide this vital facility frequently relay instructions relating to thousands of pounds of bookmakers' covering money, all of which has to be suitably invested in the last few frantic minutes before the 'off'.

Incidentally, the large bookmaking multiples, especially Ladbrokes, channel large sums taken in their licensed betting offices back to the course to bolster up what in recent years has often become a rather weak 'live' market. Since such practices can radically distort the course market, some professionals have been heard to complain that prices quoted against some runners do not reflect their real value, merely what many members of the public, rather arbitrarily, are up to in the many betting shops of a bookmaking multiple. Indeed, such off-course betting behaviour may differ radically from what has been happening at the meeting itself. What is undeniable is that 'blower activity' or 'office support' in the branches of large bookmakers can, on occasion, radically change the course market, as the following betting return indicates:

Shiny Hour ended at 7–2, having disputed early favouritism at 9–2 with Golden Spray and Pass No Remarks who lengthened to 5–1 and 11–2 respectively, a better order being Drago, 5–1 to 4–1. Kiki Mouse figured at 5–1 and 11–2, Singularity easing 6–1 to 8–1, Trust Sally and Phantom Flyer from around 12–1 to 16–1 and Sammy Waters 14–1 to 20–1. A rush of late office, 'Blower' and general business saw Naughty Twinkle drop rapidly from 25–1 to 9–1.

The signalling methods employed by tic-tacs and the ways in which agents of large concerns channel covering money into the course market are naturally confidential and impossible for the uninitiated to decode. They are quite different from the much more public system that is used to relay market information and to transmit wagers from bookmakers in one enclosure on the racecourse to another. The tic-tacs these activities involve will be at their most conspicuous high in the main grandstand in Tattersalls' enclosure. These are the so-called 'top men'. They are expert operators and send market prices and information (signalled up to them by colleagues in the main betting ring) out to bookmakers operating in the cheaper course enclosures. They also relay bets sent to them from tic-tacs operating in these relatively remote areas who work for 'course' bookmakers whose limited capital makes them understandably anxious, on occasion, to lay off the excessive liabilities they can incur on certain runners.

These so-called 'top men' in many ways act as general betting liaison officers and thus do much to stabilise prices all over the racecourse. They also alert bookmakers to important betting developments. For example, if there has been heavy off-course support for a particular runner (such as Naughty Twinkle in the betting return shown), the activity involved will be 'trumpeted' to the trade by the top man signalling (see previous page).

This is something that as a racegoer you should watch out for since it will help you to establish the source of any market support you witness and to assess its significance. Before the actual signals relating to odds and bets that tic-tacs send to each other are examined in detail, you need to be aware that since these take standard and highly 'public' forms that can be interpreted, the identities of the animals to which they relate are kept confidential through the use of a special bookmakers' racecard or 'twist' card. It is not generally known that this document lists runners in the strictly alphabetical way in which their names always appear on the bookmakers' boards. Thus, when a tic-tac wishes to pass on information about horse No. 4 for example, he is referring to a runner which is unlikely (except by coincidence) to have been allotted this number in the official racecard and to be carrying it on a weightcloth. A page from one such 'twist' card (suitably inscribed by a tic-tac with details of betting fluctuations) is illustrated on page 142, before an example of newspaper coverage of the race in question.

The illustration on pages 142/3 shows that even when, on occasion, the runners in some non-handicaps are listed alphabetically on both the racecard used by bookmakers and that sold by the racecourse executive, these two cards remain radically different. This is because only one – that of the bookmaker – is printed late enough for its numbering system to be confined to horses that have actually been declared to run at the over-night stage; in contrast, the numbers given on official racecards, whether they relate to an alphabetical listing of runners or not, will never be successive since some relating to horses originally enumerated as runners at the penultimate declaration stage will be conspicuously absent. Incidentally, if any runner is withdrawn after the over-night stage (eg. Meet in the Casbah on page 144) its name is deleted from the twist card and on no account are any potentially confusing changes made to the numbers shown against the remaining runners.

7–45

1 ALBA LE 12 14 12 10 8 10
2 ALSIRAT 16 20 25
3 GEMMERLY JANE 10 7 8
4 INTEGRATION 6 7 8
5 JIMMYFISHER 8 14 20
6 LIGHTVALE 6 8 10 12
7 LITTLE BILSHAM 7 8
8 LUCKY TESS 10 12 20
9 MOUNTAIN LAD 16 20
10 MR ESKIMO 16 33
11 PARITY 14 20
12 PRECIPITOUS 6 8 7
13 ROYAL ROUSSEL 16 20
14 SARS BROOK 12 20
15 SIR BRYN 4 4½ 4 3/2
16 SPARTAN CHOICE –6 25 33
18 STOURHEAD 20 25 33
19 THE DRUNKEN DUCK 4 4½ 4 3/2

1 40342 **ALBA LEE** I R Jones 8-12-0 ... **M Williams (7)**
2 2-42244 **ALSIRAT** M Wood 10-12-0 .... **P Hewes (7)**
6 000/ **GEMMERLY JANE** Mrs J Watts 7-12-0
Miss C Perkins (7)
8 00-12F3 **INTEGRATION** E Retter 7-12-0 .... **G Cann**
9 42-430 **JIMMYFISHER** P Mann 10-12-0 ..... **P Mann (7)**
10 P-02321 **LIGHTVALE** R Case 7-12-0 ....**T Moore (7)**
11 F **LITTLE BILSHAM** Mrs G Spratt 7-12-0 **J Bryan (7)**
12 0P0/V3-1 **LUCKY TESS** G Tregaskes 8-12-0 **S Andrews (7)**
13 U24-23 **MEET IN THE CASBAH** H Manners 8-12-0
A J Wilson
15 F020-00 **MOUNTAIN LAD** J Cooper 9-12-0 ......**D Kinsella**
16 P32F3P **MR ESKIMO** J Wade 10-12-0 ..... **E McIntyre (4)**
17 4F/10 **PARITY (BF)** Mrs A Holman 10-12-0
Mrs A Holman (7)
18 F1F211 **PERSIAN SCIMITAR** Mrs V Robinson 8-12-0 ——
DOUBTFUL
19 33U221 **PRECIPITOUS** Mrs J Bainbridge 9-12-0
Miss A Dare (7)
21 2P **ROYAL ROUSSEL** F Loggins 8-12-0 ..... **A Hill (7)**
22 01U **SARS BROOK** C Arrand 9-12-0 ....**N Tully (7)**
23 00000/1 **SIR BRYN** E Linnell 7-12-0 ....**G Tarry (7)**
24 P4P-00P **SPARTAN CHOICE** Miss M Preece 9-12-0
J Pritchard (7)
25 **STOURHEAD** C Green 10-12-0 ......**N Mitchell (7)**
26 3-22102 **THE DRUNKEN DUCK** B Munro-Wilson 8-12-0
B Munro-Wilson (7)
Probable S.P.: 2 Meet in the Casbah, 3 The Drunken Duck, 4 Alsirat, 6 Alba Le, Little Rilsham, 12 Sir Bryn.

(Reproduced by kind permission of 'The Daily Mail')

To alert his colleagues to the fact that he is about to transmit information, a tic-tac will firstly give the following call sign:

He will then indicate the number of the runner on the twist card about which he has something to convey by means of signals that form part of a complete tic-tac system known as 'Pineys'. This features separate signs for the first five cardinal numbers and also the tenth. There are no single signs for the numbers 6, 7, or 8. As can be seen from the third line of the following illustration, these particular numbers are signalled as 5 followed by the sign for 1, 2, or 3.

2 or 2/1

2
Bottle.

3 or 3/1

3
Carpet/tres/gimmel

4 or 4/1

5 or 5/1

6 or 6/1

Exes.
X's, Tom mix, Half a Stretch

7 or 7/1

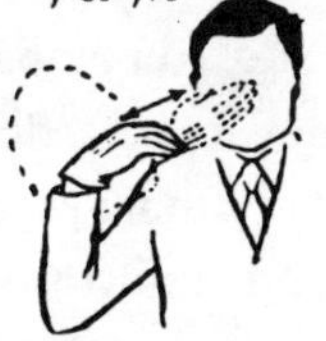

Neves. Nevis.

8 or 8/1

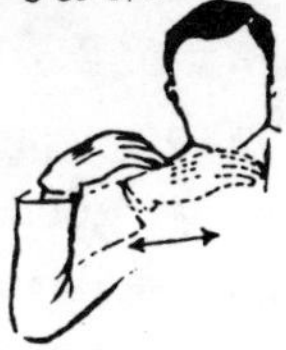

T.H.

9 or 9/1

Enin.
Teapot handle

If the tic-tac wishes to refer to a horse that has been given a high number on his twist card (for example No. 21), he will give the signal for 10, quickly repeat it, and then signal the sign for 1 as follows:

There is, naturally, provision made in Pineys for the passing on of prices and the striking of wagers. The following chart shows the many other single and composite signs that are used to broadcast betting information from bookmaker to bookmaker. It includes the colourful terms for various rates of odds that form a large part of the parlance of the 'layers'. It should be noted that the first sign illustrated, the 'no offer' signal, relates to a particular animal on which, usually for a very good reason, bookmakers are initially unwilling to trade. A tic-tac will pass on this signal to the minor betting enclosures if bookmakers in the main ring are declining at the start of trading to take bets on a particular runner which they know, via their extensive 'intelligence service', will justifiably play a prominent, if not a leading, part in the market. By failing to quote a price against this 'feared' runner, bookmakers can lure money away from it in the opening exchanges, especially if they make a great show of laying another runner against the field, thereby suggesting that it is the undisputed favourite. The price this 'false' favourite is initially given invariably lengthens when the so-called 'wait horse' eventually receives a market quotation.

NO OFFER

ODDS ON

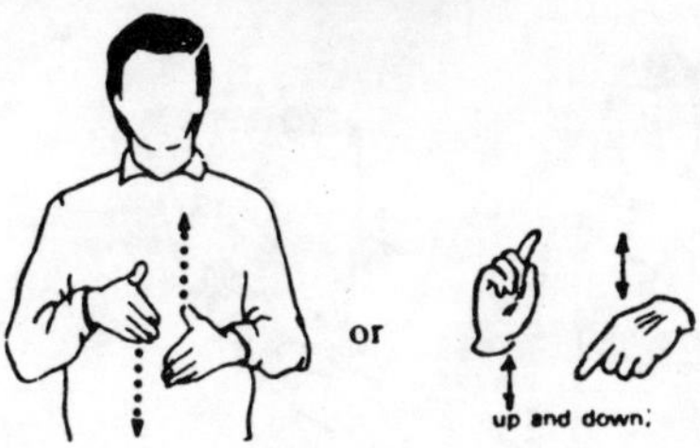

Evens: Scotch/one to one/levels.

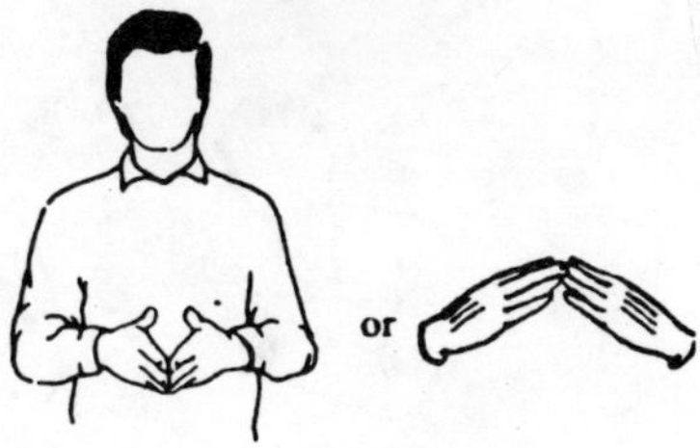

11–10: Tips/bits.

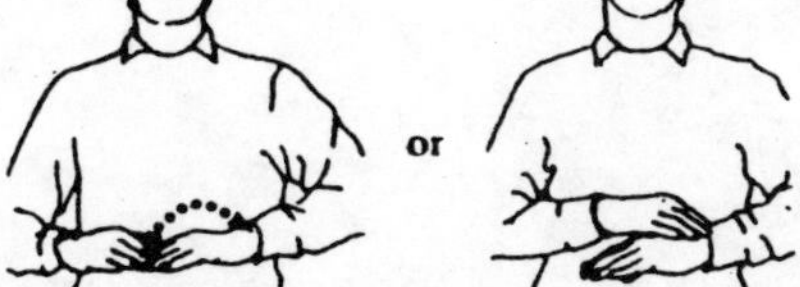

6–5: Sais a ching.

5–4: Wrist/hand to rouf.

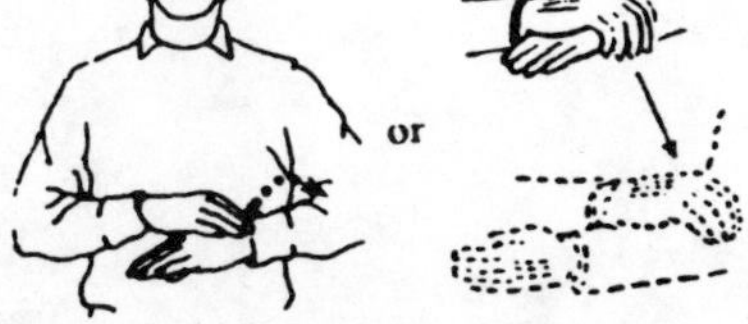

11–8: Up the arm.

or

or

Shoulder/neves
to rouf.

7–4

or

15–8: Double shoulder/double taps

9–4

Top of the head/enin to rouf
Top of the Crust

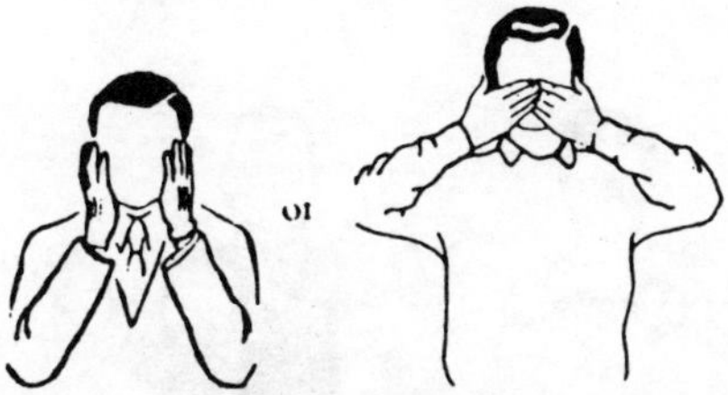

5–2: Face/bottle and a half.

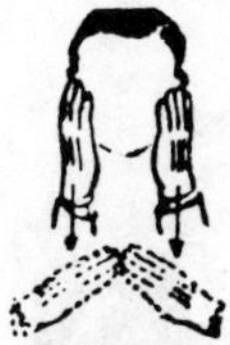

11–4: Elef a vier.

100–30: Scruffy and dirty.
Three and a bit.

7–2: Carpet and a half.

9–2: Shoulders/rouf and a half.

33–1: Double carpet

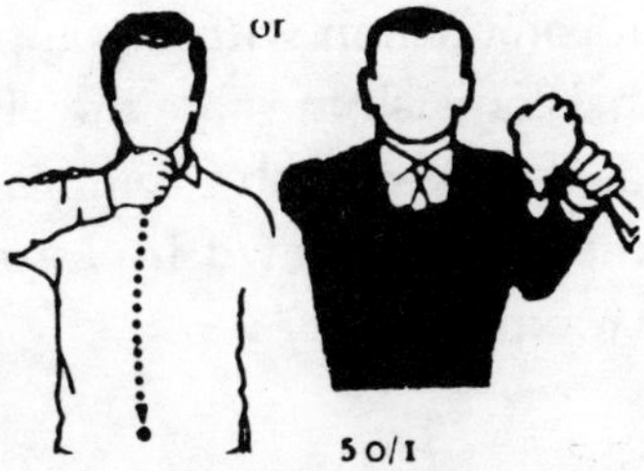

50/1

MAKING A BET

100/1
Long-Un

FINISH

As can be seen from the the illustration above, Pineys also allows for the passing of bets by tic-tacs on behalf of the bookmakers who employ them. Finally, there is one further tic-tac signal to which particular attention should be paid. It is signalled as follows:

This is used in conjunction with the appropriate twist card number when bookmakers wish to share the vital information that well-known professional backers, stable commissioners, particularly astute owners or trainers or shrewd investors have been seen supporting a particular runner.

STRATEGY 31

Avoiding Pitfalls and Seizing Opportunities

Before advice is given on which money really does talk in racing, I think it worth sounding a note of caution. My research when I was 'Centaur', the market correspondent of *Racing Monthly*, proved conclusively that only around 15% of all contractions in the betting actually involve winning horses and indicated that this market presents many pitfalls for the unwary. These can be avoided if you adopt certain procedures and are aware of some of the 'come-ons' by which bookmakers sometimes attempt to persuade the unwary to part with their cash. In general, just as you should always bet within your means and purchase something of quality if its price is appealing, so on the turf you should invest only what you can afford to lose. You should take account not only of the odds on offer, but also use objective criteria of selection to assess whether a wager is an attractive proposition. Indeed, betting can be thought of as similar to bargain hunting. You should consider value for money and either bet promptly because 'you feel' the odds are unlikely to remain at favourable levels for long, or wait to see whether they reach rates that you think represent good value.

However, when a bet is contemplated, just as when you are shopping, caution needs to be exercised. Indeed, it is wise to consider whether you are being offered too great a 'bargain' about a horse which, rather ironically, the compilers of newspaper forecasts of starting prices or ante-post bookmakers led you to expect, as a leading market fancy, would start at several rates below the odds actually on offer in the market. The following 'ladder of odds' will readily enable the backer to gauge the size of such a disparity.

LADDER OF ODDS

100–1	11–2	8–11
66–1	5–1	4–6
50–1	9–2	8–13
40–1	4–1	4–7
33–1	7–2	8–15
25–1	100–30	1–2
22–1	3–1	4–9
20–1	11–4	40–95
19–1	5–2	2–5
18–1	95–40	4–11
17–1	9–4	1–3
16–1	2–1	30–100
15–1	15–8	2–7
14–1	7–4	1–4
13–1	13–8	2–9
12–1	6–4	1–5
11–1	11–8	2–11
10–1	5–4	1–6
9–1	6–5	2–13
8–1	11–10	1–7
15–2	Evens	2–15
7–1	10–11	1–8
13–2	5–6	
6–1	4–5	

It is, of course, even more disconcerting if what you regard as a suspiciously high opening rate then drifts alarmingly, fails to 'harden' or is trimmed by such a small percentage as to remain out of line by three or more rates of odds with what was forecast. Naturally, it is no more difficult to detect such a disturbing disparity between the forecast and the actual prices quoted against your selection than it is to discover a total lack of interest in its chances in the market. If the odds do not move as you expect then you have several options. You may decide to rely totally and fearlessly on what you feel is your superior judgement, or alternatively, infer from what is happening in the market that your selection is unworthy of support. One way of resolving this dilemma, which is made acute by the sobering conclusion of extensive surveys into starting prices that show that nearly three-quarters of races are won by horses who figure in the first three in the betting, might be to compromise by staking a small amount to win on a horse whose odds reach levels well beyond what your calculations suggest is appropriate.

In order to ensure that you place your bet at the most opportune moment, you must be ready to take advantage of the few 'bargain' rates that remain on some tardy bookmakers' boards if the odds about your fancy are finally 'taken' and then start to contract in the ring. Such movement in the market, which at least offers some reassurance and the hope that it may well prove significant, will invariably be first seen in Tattersalls' enclosure on the boards of bookmakers trading nearest the rails beyond which the members' enclosure is located. Thus, shrewd racegoers position themselves so that they can quickly observe such a development and, even more crucially, perceive precisely where, away from the rails down the line of layers in Tattersalls, they can still find the value price. You must lose no time in taking this price before it is wiped away by a particular bookmaker (known disparagingly as a 'dentist' in the trade), who, probably because he is not paying for the services of a tic-tac, is one price adrift of his colleagues.

There are other less dramatic ways of determining when to bet. Firstly, it is always advisable to calculate from the opening show on their boards the percentage to which bookmakers are initially working; provided that the calculation involved (already described) takes in the various odds quoted against all the runners, it will indicate whether or not those laying the odds are likely to become more generous in their future dealings. Frequently, you will find that bookmakers (who work to marked cards indicating by means of a cross, a dot and a capital c, the likely first and second favourites and a third runner about which they are warned to be 'careful') recognise their initial vulnerability and so start to trade at rates that are distinctly ungenerous. The opening show will often feature prices that prove to be 'over-round' by well over 20%. If this is the case, I suggest that you refer to the 'ladder' and patiently note the opening prices, record the possible significant extents by which some may be higher or lower than forecast rates, and hope for some overall improvement in the trading position. This will often occur, as is illustrated in the table on page 159 which shows exactly how the odds quoted against the runners in an eight horse race fluctuated between the first 'show' and the close of trading.

Horse	Odds in First Betting Show	Percentage Equivalent	Odds in Final Betting Show	Percentage Equivalent
A	4–7	63.64	4–5	55.56
B	7–2	22.22	9–2	18.18
C	5–1	16.67	7–1	12.50
D	5–1	16.67	9–1	10.00
E	16–1	5.88	12–1	7.67
F	16–1	5.88	25–1	3.85
G	16–1	5.88	25–1	3.85
H	20–1	4.76	33–1	2.94
	Total	141.60	Total	114.55
	Over-round	41.60	Over-round	14.55

Bookmakers, of course, can only exercise total control over their opening prices. This is because these particular rates which have been 'floated' in a speculative fashion will obviously, as soon as actual betting commences, either contract or lengthen according to demand for them or the lack of it amongst the racing public. What I think is more important to note, however, is that there are some significant exceptions to this rule. These deviations which are so familiar to the wily professional actually involve bogus market moves made by bookmakers to persuade the unwary to part with their cash and so bring in some trade when business is slack.

The first of these concerns a 'floorman' whose job it is to keep an eye on prices and to place bets or 'hedge' for the bookmaker who employs him. On occasion, this particular person may be heard recommending in a loud and hardly confidential manner that his employer reduce, as a matter of some urgency, a particular rate of odds that is showing on his board. Such 'flimping' as it is known in the trade, whereby an attempt is made to persuade a backer to accept a price which is about to be extended or can be bettered elsewhere, is a well-known 'come-on'.

Another confidence trick which the professional backer seldom swallows involves a large 'blue', yet actually bogus, bet being struck, again all too noisily and flamboyantly, about a particular runner. Gullible members of the public, on witnessing this, may imagine that the 'investor' involved is a confident professional or inspired stable commissioner or a practically shrewd operator. They may be lured to rush forward and follow his example, only to find that the odds in question have been unfairly trimmed by the time they come to place their own bets.

A third apparently significant 'contraction' in the odds that you should wisely suspect involves an outsider whose longish odds the bookmakers trim by a point or two in an attempt to deflect backers away from both a first and second favourite which have already found support in the market. This is one of the ways in which they encourage those many sporting or greedy racegoers who search for outsiders on which to place their smallish stakes in the understandable, but often forlorn, hope that they will somehow defeat horses with outstanding claims. Conversely, of course, when it is only an outsider's odds which contract and when they do so by a substantial percentage, you should be left in no doubt as to the authenticity of the betting movement that is involved. Indeed, you should regard this as highly significant.

The following race return is a case in point:

2493 VODATA NURSERY £6368.00 (£1904.00: £912.00: £416.00). **7f** 3-45 (3-47)
(Weights raised 10 lb)

2002^{3} **Pay Homage** *(IABalding)* 9-4 SCauthen (8) (3rd st: plld out over 2f out: led over 1f out: drvn out) .... —1
2078^{4} Port Vauban *(RHannon)* 8-7 ‡^{3}DaleGibson (3) (5th st: hmpd over 2f out: hdwy over 1f out: r.o ins fnl f) 3.2
2445^{2} Almasa *(JCFox)* 9-2 JWilliams (5) (hdwy over 2f out: ev ch over 1f out: nt qckn) .. 2½.3
2255* Sipsi Fach (Jt-Fav) *(MBell)* 8-5 ‡^{7}JWeaver (6) (4th st: led 3f out tl over 1f out: one pce) ½.4
1385* Sir Bancroft *(HJCollingridge)* 8-13 JQuinn (4) (6th st: r.o one pce fnl 2f) ¾.5
2094^{3} Greenhills Lad (IRE) *(RAkehurst)* 8-10 JReid (1) (lw: nvr nr to chal) hd.6
2313^{3} Mamalama *(LJHolt)* 8-0 TyroneWilliams (7) (hdwy over 2f out: hung rt over 1f out; wknd fnl f) 5.7
2106* Leitrim Pride *(GLewis)* 9-7 PatEddery (2) (lw: w ldr: 2nd st: rdn & wknd 2f out) 1½.8
1872^{3} Golden General *(WGRWightman)* 8-2 RFox (9) (s.s: a bhd) 5.9
2131* Whippers Delight (IRE) (Jt-Fav) *(JPerry)* 8-5 WCarson (10) (led 4f) 5.10

4/1 Sipsi Fach, Whippers Delight (IRE), **13/2** Leitrim Pride, **15/2** PAY HOMAGE(12/1—7/1), **8/1** Almasa, **10/1** Sir Bancroft, **12/1** Mamalama(op 8/1), **14/1** Greenhills Lad (IRE), **16/1** Ors. CSF £96.82, CT £864.08. Tote £7.20: £2.10 £5.80 £2.80 (£121.20). Miss A. V. Hill (KINGSCLERE) bred by Cheveley Park Stud Ltd. 10Rn
1m 28.24 (2.94)
SF—39/19/20/7/13/9

Source: Raceform Handicap Book

As can be seen clearly above, the market move for the horse sent to Goodwood to run during the annual British holiday of its owner, Paul Mellon, by its trainer, Ian Balding, was from 12–1 to 15–2. This was highly significant, given the total lack of support, once the betting had opened, for any other runner in the Vodata Nursery! Again, if you see that only one of two market leaders (preferably the favourite since mere possession of this exalted status is usually sufficient to produce a great deal of imitative, as opposed to inspired, support) has its odds only marginally trimmed and an outsider has its odds cut considerably, the latter development can often provide a profitable pointer. Another race return well illustrates this point.

2598 **Cookham Claiming Stakes £2,755 6f.** (2:45)

	NIKKI DOW 3-8-4 G Duffield (1) *led 2 and a half fs out, sn clr, jst hld on*	(8 to 1 op 12 to 1 tchd 14 to 1)	1
2184	GREEN DOLLAR 6-9-2 G Bardwell (23) *chsd ldrs, hrd rdn wl o'r one furlong out, str run fnl furlong, jst fld.*	(7 to 2 fav op 4 to 1 tchd 3 to 1)	2
1958^{6}	RIVIERA SCENE 6-8-3 (7*) T Sprake (13) *al prmnt, ev ch o'r 2 fs out, drvn and one pace fnl furlong*	(9 to 1 op 10 to 1 tchd 12 to 1)	3
2373	SAALIB 6-8-7 J Reid (17) *prmnt, ev ch 2 fs out, one pace und str pres*	(25 to 1 op 20 to 1 tchd 33 to 1)	4
1839	FIRST TRADITION 4-8-5 I Johnson (15) *chsd ldrs, hrd rdn 2 fs out, unbl to quicken*	(16 to 1 op 12 to 1)	5
452^{8}	DEEPWOOD NANUSKET 3-7-4 (5*) Dale Gibson (18) *hndy o'r 4 fs, no extr*	(7 to 1 op 6 to 1)	6
1778^{7}	SUNGROVE PRIDE 3-8-0 C Rutter (10) *nvr better plcd*	(33 to 1)	7
1567^{8}	BATCHWORTH DANCER 4-9-6 (3*) J Quinn (21) *outpcd frm hfwy.*	(20 to 1 op 25 to 1)	8
1939	LUAGA 3-8-8 R Cochrane (14) *nvr dngrs*	(33 to 1)	9
	ITS SMITHY 3-8-5 P Cook (9) *nvr on terms*	(20 to 1 op 14 to 1)	10
1893	THATCHED MILL 3-8-2^{2} T Quinn (19) *nvr dngrs.*	(16 to 1 op 14 to 1 tchd 20 to 1)	11
2349^{3}	PRINCE OF TIDES 3-8-11 B Rouse (20) *nvr dngrs.*	(17 to 2 op 8 to 1 tchd 9 to 1)	12
2346^{2}	LOCHTILLUM 10-8-11 T Williams (12) *nvr dngrs.*	(14 to 1 op 12 to 1)	13
1830	MAJOR JACKO 6-8-7 (7*) P J Maher (6) *outpcd*	(33 to 1)	0
1954	KATIE SCARLETT 3-8-2 N Adams (4) *speed o'r 4 fs.*	(20 to 1 op 16 to 1 tchd 25 to 1)	0
2217^{7}	RUMBOOGIE 5-8-11 (7*) R Price (5) *in tch 4 fs*	(33 to 1)	0
1916^{9}	FLYING ROOFER 3-7-12 A Proud (3) *outpcd*	(33 to 1)	0
2244^{8}	CHRISTMAS HOLS (bl) 3-8-3 (7*) A Morris (2) *in tch to hfwy.*	(33 to 1)	0
1954^{8}	MEZZAPA 3-7-7 (7*) C Avery (22) *outpcd*	(33 to 1)	0
2110^{4}	WINGED MELODY 3-8-12 Pat Eddery (7) *led 3 and a half fs, sn btn.*	(10 to 1 op 8 to 1)	0
2207	ALL HONESTY (bl) 4-9-0 B Raymond (8) *prmnt till broke blood vessel and collapsed o'r 2 fs out*	(20 to 1 op 33 to 1)	f
2308^{5}	ROYSIA BOY (bl) 9-8-11 W Carson (11) *sn rdn alng, beh frm hfwy.*	(12 to 1 op 10 to 1 tchd 14 to 1)	22

Dist: Hd, 3l, 1½l, 3l, sht-hd, 2½l, ½l, 1l, 1½l, hd. 1m 10.60s. b 0.80s (22 Ran).
SR: 34/45/27/18/4/-/ (G D Waters), Sir Mark Prescott

Source: From The Weekender

As can readily be seen, of the two market leaders, the favourite Green Dollar 'contracted' by only 13%, in shortening from 4–1 to 7–2, while Deepwood Nanusket drifted as the second favourite. In contrast, as the following 'betting reference tables' will show, the newcomer Nikki Dow advanced in the betting 'against' his opening odds of 12–1 to 8–1 – a large and most significant contraction of 33% that transpired by virtue, not of the imitative behaviour that so characterises the backers of market leaders, but because of the very heavy weight of genuinely inspired support for this 'debutant'.

Figures showing Proportionate Extents (expressed as percentages) to which Odds contract to reach lower rates

100-1 to	66-1	33%
	50-1	50%
66-1 to	50-1	24%
	40-1	39%
	33-1	50%
50-1 to	40-1	20%
	33-1	33%
	25-1	50%
40-1 to	33-1	18%
	25-1	38%
	22-1	45%
	20-1	50%
33-1 to	25-1	25%
	22-1	33%
	20-1	39%
	19-1	43%
	18-1	46%
	17-1	51%
	16-1	52%
25-1 to	22-1	12%
	20-1	20%
	19-1	24%
	18-1	28%
	17-1	32%
	16-1	36%
	15-1	40%
	14-1	44%
	13-1	48%
	12-1	52%
20 1 to	19-1	5%
	18-1	10%
	17-1	15%
	16-1	20%
	15-1	25%
	14-1	30%
	13-1	35%
	12-1	40%
	11-1	45%
	10-1	50%
19 1 to	18-1	5%
	17 1	10%
	16-1	16%
	15-1	22%
	14-1	26%
	13-1	32%
	12-1	37%
	10-1	47%
	9-1	53%
18 1 to	17 1	5%
	16-1	11%
	15-1	17%
	14-1	22%
	13-1	28%
	12-1	33%
18-1 to	11-1	39%
"	10-1	44%
"	9-1	50%
17-1 to	16-1	6%
"	15-1	12%
"	14-1	18%
"	13-1	24%
"	12-1	29%
"	11-1	35%
"	10-1	41%
"	9-1	47%
"	8-1	53%
16-1 to	15-1	6%
"	14-1	12%
"	13-1	19%
"	12-1	25%
"	11-1	31%
"	10-1	38%
"	9-1	44%
"	8-1	50%
15-1 to	14-1	7%
"	13-1	16%
"	12-1	20%
"	11-1	27%
"	10-1	33%
"	9-1	40%
"	8-1	47%
"	15-2	50%
14-1 to	13-1	7%
"	12-1	14%
"	11-1	21%
"	10-1	29%
"	9-1	36%
"	8-1	43%
"	15-2	47%
"	7-1	50%
13-1 to	12-1	8%
"	11-1	15%
"	10-1	23%
"	9-1	31%
"	8-1	38%
"	15-2	42%
"	7-1	46%
"	13-2	50%
12-1 to	11-1	8%
"	10-1	17%
"	9-1	25%
"	8-1	33%
"	15-2	37%
"	7-1	42%
"	13-2	46%
"	6-1	50%
11-1 to	10-1	9%
"	9-1	18%
11-1 to	8-1	27%
"	15-2	32%
"	7-1	36%
"	13-2	41%
"	6-1	45%
"	11-2	50%
10-1 to	9-1	10%
"	8-1	20%
"	15-2	25%
"	7-1	30%
"	13-2	35%
"	6-1	40%
"	11-2	45%
"	5-1	50%
9-1 to	8-1	11%
"	15-2	16%
"	7-1	22%
"	13-2	28%
"	6-1	33%
"	11-2	39%
"	5-1	44%
"	9-2	50%
8-1 to	7-1	12%
"	13-2	19%
"	6-1	25%
"	11-2	31%
"	5-1	37%
"	9-2	44%
"	4-1	50%
7-1 to	13-2	8%
"	6-1	14%
"	11-2	22%
"	5-1	29%
"	9-2	36%
"	4-1	43%
"	7-2	50%
13-2 to	6-1	8%
"	11-2	16%
"	5-1	23%
"	9-2	31%
"	4-1	38%
"	7-2	46%
"	100-30	49%
"	3-1	54%
6-1 to	11-2	8%
"	5-1	17%
"	9-2	25%
"	4-1	33%
"	7-2	42%
"	100-30	45%
"	3-1	50%
11-2 to	5-1	9%
"	9-2	18%
"	4-1	27%
"	7-2	36%
"	100-30	40%
"	3-1	45%
"	11-4	50%
5-1 to	9-2	10%
"	4-1	20%

5-1	to	7-2	30%
"		100-30	33%
"		3-1	40%
"		11-4	45%
"		5-2	50%
9-2	to	4-1	11%
"		7-2	22%
"		100-30	27%
"		3-1	33%
"		11-4	39%
"		5-2	44%
"		95-40	48%
"		9-4	50%
4-1	to	7-2	13%
"		100-30	18%
"		3-1	25%
"		11-4	31%
"		5-2	38%
"		95-40	41%
"		9-4	44%
"		2-1	50%
7-2	to	100-30	6%
"		3-1	14%
"		11-4	21%
"		5-2	29%
"		95-40	33%
"		9-4	36%
"		2-1	43%
"		15-8	46%
"		7-4	50%
100-30	to	3-1	10%
"		11-4	18%
"		5-2	25%
"		95-40	30%
"		9-4	33%
"		2-1	40%
"		15-8	44%
"		7-4	48%
"		13-8	49%
"		6.4	55%
3-1	to	11-4	9%
"		5-2	17%
"		95-40	22%
"		9-4	25%
"		2-1	34%
"		15-8	38%
"		7-4	42%
"		13-8	46%
"		6-4	50%
11-4	to	5-2	10%
"		95-40	15%
"		9-4	19%
"		2-1	28%
"		15-8	32%
"		7-4	37%
"		13-8	42%
"		6-4	46%
"		11-8	49%
5-2	to	95-40	6%
"		9-4	10%
5-2	to	2-1	20%
		15-8	26%
		7-4	30%
		13-8	36%
		6-4	40%
		11-8	46%
		5-4	50%
95-40	to	9-4	5%
		2-1	15%
		15-8	21%
		7-4	26%
		13-8	32%
		6-4	37%
		11-8	42%
		5-4	47%
		6-5	49%

9-4	to	2-1	12%
		15-8	17%
		7-4	23%
"		13-8	28%
"		6-4	34%
"		11-8	40%
"		5-4	45%
"		6-5	47%
"		11-10	52%
2-1	to	15-8	6%
		7-4	7%
"		13-8	13%
"		6-4	19%
"		11-8	25%
"		5-4	32%
"		6-5	38%
"		11-10	40%
"		evens	50%
15-8	to	7-4	6%
"		13-8	13%
"		6-4	20%
		11-8	27%
"		5-4	33%
"		6-5	36%
"		11-10	41%
"		evens	47%
		10-11	51%
7-4	to	13-8	7%
"		6-4	14%
"		11-8	21%
"		5-4	29%
"		6-5	31%
"		11-10	37%
"		evens	43%
"		10-11	48%
"		5-6	53%
13-8	to	6.4	8%
"		11-8	15%
"		5-4	23%
"		6-5	26%
"		11-10	32%
"		evens	38%
"		10-11	44%
"		5-6	49%
13-8	to	4-5	51%
6-4	to	11-8	8%
"		5-4	17%
"		6-5	20%
"		11-10	27%
"		evens	33%
"		10-11	39%
"		5-6	45%
"		4-5	47%
"		8-11	52%
11-8	to	5-4	9%
"		6-5	13%
"		11-10	20%
"		evens	27%
"		10-11	34%
"		5-6	40%
"		4-5	42%
"		8-11	47%
"		4-6	52%
5-4	to	6-5	4%
"		11-10	12%
"		evens	20%
"		10-11	27%
"		5-6	34%
"		4-5	36%
"		8-11	42%
"		4-6	47%
"		8-13	51%
6-5	to	11-10	8%
"		evens	17%
"		10-11	24%
"		5-6	31%

"		4-5	33%
"		8-11	39%
"		4-6	44%
"		8-13	49%
"		4-7	52%
11-10	to	evens	9%
"		10-11	17%
"		5-6	25%
"		4-5	27%
"		8-11	34%
"		4-6	39%
"		8-13	44%
"		4-7	48%
"		8-15	52%
evens	to	10-11	9%
"		5-6	17%
"		4-5	20%
"		8-11	27%
"		4-6	33%
"		8-13	38%
"		4-7	43%
"		8-15	47%
"		1-2	50%
10-11	to	5-6	9%
"		4-5	12%
"		8-11	20%
"		4-6	27%
"		8-13	32%
10-11	to	4-7	37%
"		8-15	41%
"		1-2	45%
"		4-9	51%
5-6	to	4-5	3%
"		8-11	12%
"		4-6	19%
"		8-13	26%
"		4-7	31%
"		8-15	35%
"		1-2	39%
"		4-9	46%
"		40-95	49%
4-5	to	8-11	8%
"		4-6	16%
"		8-13	22%
"		4-7	29%
"		8-15	34%
"		1-2	37%
"		40-85	41%
"		4-9	45%
"		2-5	50%
8-11	to	4-6	8%
"		8-13	15%
"		4-7	22%
"		8-15	27%
"		1-2	32%
"		40-85	36%
"		4-9	40%
"		2-5	45%
"		4-11	50%
4-6	to	8-13	7%
"		4-7	15%
"		8-15	21%
"		1-2	25%
"		40-85	36%
"		4-9	34%
"		2-5	40%
"		4-11	46%
"		1-3	51%
8-13	to	4-7	8%
"		8-15	15%
"		1-2	19%
"		40-85	24%
"		4-9	29%
"		2-5	35%
"		4-11	42%
"		1-3	47%

	(30-100)	
"	2-7	52%
4-7 to	8-15	7%
"	1-2	12%
"	40-85	18%
"	4-9	23%
"	2-5	30%
"	4-11	37%
"	1-3	42%
	(30-100)	
"	2-7	50%
8-15 to	1-2	6%
"	40-85	11%
"	4-9	17%
"	2-5	25%
"	4-11	32%
"	1-3	38%
	(30-100)	
"	2-7	45%
"	1-4	53%
1-2 to	40-85	6%
"	4-9	12%
"	2-5	20%
"	4-11	28%
"	1-3	33%
	(30-100)	
"	2-7	42%
"	1-4	50%
40-85 to	4-9	6%
"	2-5	15%
"	4-11	23%
"	1-3	30%
	(30-100)	
"	2-7	38%
"	1-4	47%
"	2-9	53%
4-9 to	2-5	9%
"	4-11	18%
"	1-3	25%
	(30-100)	
"	2-7	34%
"	1-4	43%
"	2-9	50%
4-11 to	1.3	8%
	(30-100)	
"	2-7	19%
"	1-4	31%
"	2-9	39%
"	1-5	44%
"	2-11	50%
30-100 to	2-7	12%
(1-3)		
"	1-4	24%
"	2-9	33%
"	1-5	39%
"	2-11	45%
"	1-6	48%
"	2-13	55%
2-7* to	1-4	14%
"	2-9	24%
"	1-5	31%
"	2-11	38%
"	1-6	41%
"	2-13	49%
"	1-7	52%

* In practice bookmakers seldom quote odds which are shorter than this particular rate.

STRATEGY 32:

Spotting Corner Horses

Another way of detecting possible significant movements in the betting market concerns so-called 'morning liners' (as betting forecasts are known in America). To exploit it you need to buy the first midday edition of an evening newspaper that has extensive racing coverage, and then note any disparities between the prices in its betting forecasts and those compiled far earlier by experts who, overnight, have been unable to take account of raceday factors which can crucially affect the outcome of races.

Many professionals feel the compilers of early editions of evening newspaper betting forecasts have an uncanny knack of veering away from a horse that the forecasters working for the national dailies have predicted will be favourite, but which, in the event, proves easy to back in the course market. The 'sharps' responsible for early editions of evening newspapers often identify as likely favourites horses which have been comparatively neglected by those who have had to work to far tighter press deadlines.

Conversely, of course, there are occasions when stable confidence for another horse (rather than anything being untoward) is all that causes a forecast favourite to fail to become the market leader. If, as a glance at detailed reports of betting activity will readily show, this confidence often proves misplaced, then the horse the off-course betting forecasters felt ought to be favourite may well win at odds which represent excellent value. Such horses often win or represent profitable place only wagers if their neglect in the market has nothing to do with any last-minute diminution of their chances, but rather to the misplaced conviction that rivals they appear to hold on form may, in fact, defeat them.

Overnight favourites in races that are seen to be rather 'hung out with the washing' in the course betting, for a reason that does not reflect their poor appearance in the paddock, are often worth considering. A spectacular example of how effective this method (which is applicable to both flat racing and jumping) can sometimes prove was once provided at York's main meeting. Three days before the 'Ebor' – its handicap highlight – a racing correspondent commented that 'Primary' was a certainty for this race since, in later handicaps, it was weighted to meet a rival on 8lb worse terms. This particular runner was not the horse – White Mill – that, despite Primary's status as 4–1 ante-post favourite and 'morning line' quote of 7–2, actually started favourite for Europe's richest handicap. The following day, Capt. Heath of the *Daily Mail* commented that, despite drifting to 6–1, Primary had been a heavily backed favourite ante-post and that his trainer had felt this one-time Classic contender was the proverbial 'handicap snip'. Primary, in fact, came home by four lengths in the colours of owner Khaled Abdulla.

STRATEGY 33:

Favourites – The Myths and the Facts

The fact that in bookmakers' parlance the favourite is known as the 'jolly' is but a reminder that there is nothing necessarily magical about this particular designation. The truth of the matter is that favourites often result from irrational, or even wayward, behaviour. In fact, there is no guarantee that market leaders actually have a good chance of winning their races. Indeed, favourites show an overall success rate of around 30% on most racecourses. Sadly, to some, the appellation of 'favourite' is so mesmeric that they suddenly rush to follow the example of those who may have installed a horse at the head of the market out of naive faith or wishful thinking, rather than for any good reason involving its past form.

I must confess that it was R. W. Griffiths – a past contributor to a systems column – who finally disabused me of any notion that the past record of favourites in a particular race provides a significant pointer to future prospects. Indeed, he put into precise words what I had long vaguely felt when he wrote that 'current rather than historic factors wield the greater influence on a contest'. For me, Griffiths seemed to 'say it all' when he pointed out that the title 'favourite' is necessarily artificial and ephemeral. Indeed, in the view of this Cardiff guru, the term 'favourite' is not an entity in its own right, but a short-term status designated to operate within the context of one race only. Thus, Griffiths convinced me that to back a favourite on historical grounds alone can be as futile as, but often more expensive than, chasing rainbows.

I do realise, however, that on many occasions a victorious favourite is the horse that is most highly rated by a private handicapper. Indeed, each season, races which by definition are of the highest class are won by outright favourites which are also obvious choices on the form book. It is not, then, that records detailing the fates of past runners in particular events have no value, but their usefulness is confined to indicating whether a particular race – possibly because of its position on the calendar, its importance and entry conditions – is worth spending time on with one's form book, or whether it is a 'trappy' event in which many past backers' interpretations of form have been to no avail. As the *Ladbroke Guide to Flat Racing* once put it 'the record of favourites is interesting as a general guide to the workings of form as a whole'.

STRATEGY 34:

Beaten Favourites

Paradoxes are always intriguing and truth in racing terms is often surprising. For example, the tag 'beaten favourite' can provide a profitable pointer rather than, as one might well expect, an indication of a runner to avoid. I have even seen a plan whose basic principle involves supporting a favourite that has previously been beaten in a far less prestigious and valuable race than that in which it is due to compete. This seemingly illogical and lunatic proceeding is one that over the years has produced several long-priced winners.

While one is wise to suspect the often dubious and sometimes far-fetched excuses that are advanced to explain away the failures of many horses to become successful market leaders (the jockey Brownie Carslake once told Edgar Wallace that his beaten nine-year-old might well improve in time), there are sometimes occasions when such failures should, for once, be forgiven or ignored. The trick, of course, is to determine when such previously disappointing runners should be forgiven for their 'lapses from grace'. This is naturally a difficult proceeding, but amongst the comments of their disappointed connections there will often be found excuses – relating to unsuitable going, distances or courses, ill-luck, or injury in running, injudicious riding, receiving an unfortunate draw, being left well behind in the early stages of a race, or being given 'too much to do' in the final stages – and such factors may mean you are prepared to excuse the horses concerned.

I also happen to share the belief of Bob Butchers (formerly 'Newsboy' of the *Daily Mirror*) that 'horses are just like people' in having their off days. Dancing Brave had one at Santa Anita (if one discounts the acclimatisation problems he faced there) and so did Greville Starkey when riding this champion colt at Epsom. Like humans too, as well as occasionally feeling (and performing) under par, horses, through too much riding, can become tired and jaded. Indeed, some supporters of beaten favourites support those whose lapses last time out (as the sequels to strings of far more impressive runs) have caused their trainers to rest them for longish spells so that they can return to the racecourse thoroughly refreshed. If such publications as *Superform* are consulted, beaten favourites that 'go well when fresh' can be identified. Often, after losing as unfit favourites, but having become fitter in the process, some runners quickly take their chances in more prestigious races. If these happen to be staged on tracks on which such runners have previously scored or over ideal distances and optimum going, they may well succeed at long odds that belie their actual chances.

It is, of course, the behaviour of particular individuals – many of them mesmerised by the seemingly magical designation of 'favourite' – that causes horses to be returned as market leaders. The blinkers of hope and optimism necessarily worn by many owners and trainers may well blind them to the possibility that other connections may have done as much, if not more, to win races and thus the confidence that installs some runners as market leaders can be naive and so misplaced. As I have repeatedly stressed, when it 'talks', not much of the money flying about in the on-course betting says anything that is significant or worth heeding.

However, if some trainers have sent out beaten favourites, you can be fairly sure that any losses these have occasioned have only been 'lent' and that suitable opportunities will soon be found for them to put some wheat back in the bin. Publications containing racing statistics will indicate the types of races in which particular trainers' favourites do well and, if any of these are unsuccessful, there may be grounds for giving them a chance to atone. It is certainly interesting that, perhaps the biggest certainty in recent seasons, Dancing Brave in the 1986 King George at Ascot, had previously been a beaten favourite.

STRATEGY 35:

Market Moves to Note

Just as market analysts very closely monitor the activities of certain stockmarket investors whose money is regarded as decidedly 'smart', so the backer should note the sources of any inspired support for winning horses. Indeed, the fact that bookmakers do not (unlike the Tote) allow the prices they quote to be completely dictated by the volume of money they take on the runners in a race, but often tailor these to the past success rates or otherwise of those wagering with them – trimming the odds of runners supported by well-known 'sharpes' or 'faces' – is yet another important reason why attention should be paid to that minority amongst horses' 'connections' who regularly make winning wagers.

One such individual is Barry Hills whose meteoric rise as a trainer has taken him to perhaps the best-equipped British training complex outside Newmarket. Hills, who was first able to set himself up as a trainer thanks to a truly golden gamble on Frankincense in the 1968 Lincoln, at that time joined other head lads in sharing, but also keeping generally dark, news of many such successful coups. If the backer can row in with the action such activity features, then so much the better.

On occasion, the placing of such 'smart' money can be dramatic, as I once noticed after I had finished reading a particularly amusing piece in a racing annual about engineering a betting coup. In this, for reasons of camouflage, the ploy of enlisting a troop of brownies, so they could canter up and down lines of racecourse bookmakers with handfuls of fivers 'to make the most of the 20's and, after they'd all gone, the 16's and then the 14's and so on', had been lightheartedly recommended. As it happened, truth in the form of some action at Market Rasen turned out to be almost stranger than this fiction since, in the very first race of a jumping season, five men, all friends and each with £500 in his pocket, set out from London for this Lincolnshire venue. Once there, the man in charge issued his instructions – to back Toukshad in the opener, but only at his given signal. At the opening show, Toukshad, trained by Roland O'Sullivan, stood at 10–1, but when the five had finished tilting at the ring, its odds were 5–4, at which rate he romped home by eight lengths.

News that this spectacular gamble had netted £115,000 came as no surprise to several citizens of O'Sullivan's home town of Bognor Regis who, before Toukshad's triumph, had found a way of making up shortfalls in their income caused by stay-away holidaymakers. This involved walking into 'The Winning Post' – a betting shop at nearby Nyetimber – and backing any of Roland's horses (that regularly walked past this establishment) if ever they were seen to attract market support at a race meeting. It is precisely this ploy – of supporting the supported runners of those responsible for the very small amount of 'talking money' that circulates in the betting ring – that the select list beginning on page 177 (of those connected with horses whose past successes have often been the sequel to market support) should facilitate.

Trainer	Possibly Significant Jockey Booking	FLAT Type of Race	Market Status	Racecourses to Especially Note (if any)
R. Akehurst	J. Reid, Pat Eddery, T. Quinn	Two-year-olds, Non-Handicaps	Favourites and Shorteners	Windsor
D. Arbuthnot	J. Williams, B. Doyle, T. Quinn	Handicaps	—	Newmarket
R. Armstrong	W. Carson, D. Harrison	Three-year-olds	Shorteners	Newbury
R. Bastiman	L. Charnock, J. Reid, H. Bastiman	Weight for Age Events	Shorteners	—
R. Boss	M. Roberts	Two-year-olds, Non-handicaps	Shorteners	Newmarket
N. Bycroft	S. Webster, S. Maconey	Two-year-olds, Handicaps	Shorteners	Hamilton
N. Callaghan	L. Dettori	Weight for Age Events	Shorteners	Lingfield
M. Camacho	S. Webster, L. Charnock, N. Conorton	Three-year-olds, Handicaps	Shorteners	—
H. Collingridge	M. Rimmer, J. Quinn	Weight for Age Events Handicaps	Shorteners	Yarmouth
T. Craig	K. Darley	Weight for Age Events	—	—
C. Cyzer	T. Ives, M. Roberts	Weight for Age Events, Handicaps, Sellers	Shorteners	Beverley, Wolverhampton

Trainer	Possibly Significant Jockey Booking	FLAT Type of Race	Market Status	Racecourses to Especially Note (if any)
D. Elsworth	C. Asmussen	Three-year-olds, Weight for Age Events	Shorteners	Windsor, Haydock York, Newmarket
P. Fielden	R. Hills	Seller, Weight for Age Events	Favourites Shorteners	—
J. Gosden	L. Dettori, M. Roberts, G. Hind	Three-year-olds Non-Handicappers	Favourites Shorteners	Leicester, Folkestone, Salisbury
P. Harris	G. Hind, Paul Eddery	Two-year-olds, Non-Handicappers	Favourites Shorteners	—
G. Harwood	A. Clark, R. Cochrane	Non-Handicappers	Favourites Shorteners	Redcar, Brighton, Sandown, Bath
W. Jarvis	M. Mills, M. Tebbut, Pat Eddery	Two-year-olds, Non-Handicappers	Favourites Shorteners	Goodwood
P. Kelleway	W. Swinburn, T. Quinn	Non-Handicappers	Favourites Shorteners	Newbury
J. King	A. McGlone	Weight for Age Events	Shorteners	Chepstow

Trainer	Possibly Significant Jockey Booking	FLAT Type of Race	Market Status	Racecourses to Especially Note (if any)
P. Makin	L. Dettori, K. Darley	Weight for Age Events,	Shorteners	Lingfield, Sandown
D. Morley	W. Carson	Weight for Age Events	Favourites Shorteners	Nottingham
M. Naughton	M. Roberts, D. Harrison A. Culhane	Weight for Age Events Handicaps	Shorteners	Newmarket, Hamilton
M. Prescott	G. Duffield	Three-year-olds, Handicaps	Shorteners	Brighton, Edinburgh, Windsor
J. Toller	J. W. Weaver	Three-year-olds, Non-Handicaps	Shortners	Newbury
J.S. Wilson	N. Connorton	Weight for Age Events	Shorteners	Hamilton
G. Wragg	M. Hills	Two-year-olds, Non-Handicaps	Shorteners	Leicester

Trainer	Possibly Significant Jockey Booking	NATIONAL HUNT Type of Race	Market Status	Racecourses to Especially Note (if any)
R. Akehurst	R. Dunwoody	Novice Hurdles	Shorteners	Stratford, Plumpton
Mrs S. Bramall	J.H. Burke	Novice Hurdles, Handicaps	Favourites Shorteners	Sedgefield
J. Edwards	N. Williamson	N. Hunt Flat Novice Hurdles	Favourites Shorteners	Bangor, Cartmel, Doncaster, Leicester, Newcastle, Newton Abbot, Stratford
D. M. Grisell	T. Grantham	Handicaps Novice Hurdles	Favourites Shorteners	Fontwell, Plumpton
D. Murray-Smith	D. Gallagher	Novice Chases	Favourites Shorteners	Plumpton, Ludlow
M. Pipe	D. Bridgwater	Novice Hurdles Selling Hurdles	Favourites Shorteners	Bangor, Chepstow, Fontwell, leicester, Market Rasen, Newton Abbot, Wolverhampton
Mrs J. Pitman	W. Marston	N. Hunt-Flat, Conditional Hurdles	Favourites Shorteners	Plumpton, Sandown, Stratford, Wincanton
O. Sherwood	M. Richards, J. Osborne	Handicap Hurdles	Favourites Shorteners	Cheltenham, Newton Abbot, Folkestone, Southwell, Towcester, Wetherby, Worcester

STRATEGY 36:

Betting Strategies

Having established the various criteria by which, on occasion, a horse can be judged to have an outstanding chance, it is time to consider how to capitalise on this situation. This really involves two considerations – how to bet and how to stake. The former issue boils down to whether to bet 'win only' or 'each-way'. Unfortunately, there is no easy solution here since the circumstances that prevail determine which of these particular ploys you should adopt.

Advocates of win only betting often argue that the vast majority of the heavy business that is booked with the major rails bookmaking firms (much of it 'on the bough' or on credit) involves win only wagers. That this has increasingly been so in modern times is partly due to restrictions imposed on each-way betting. In the 'good old days' when place odds of one quarter of quite generous starting prices were generally available, it was often possible to bank on the belief that one, two or even three carefully selected horses (possibly two-year-olds unsoured by their short experience of racing) were very likely to be placed in races with eight runners – the optimum number for each-way wagering. Since then much has changed, but the modern professional or keen amateur backer should take more than a nostalgic interest in the benefits of each-way betting. This is because, despite the paltry one-fifth of its starting price that is currently paid on a horse placed in a sizeable field and the punitive burden of current off-course betting taxes, there are still circumstances when this particular form of betting is advisable.

Firstly, it is important to appreciate when not to bet each-way. Indeed, it is generally sheer folly to do so in any race – particularly a handicap – with a large field. After all, such an open contest is, by definition, expressly designed to equalise the winning chances of all its runners and indeed, in practice, often features a finish which pays handsome compliment to the skill of the handicapper. Thus, it is reasonable to subject a handicap to the strictly statistical hypothesis, based on probability theory, that any of its runners has an equal chance of winning. If such a race has attracted 27 runners, for example, then, according to this theory, any of them could be said to have a 26–1 chance of victory and one of 24–3, or 8–1, of being placed. Obviously, 8–1 is a far better rate of place odds than the 26–1/5, or slightly better than 5–1, that a bookmaker would offer, provided, of course, he were actually so foolhardy and as unbusinesslike as to allow one's selection to start, like all of its opponents, at the generously 'fair' price of 26–1. This would be the price that the theory of probability, rather than his trading instinct, would regard as appropriate. Thus, it should become clear that each-way betting at the unfairly 'over-round' odds that are usually quoted against horses running in large handicaps or other very open races with sizeable fields is, quite contrary to popular belief, against the backer's best interests.

Another common yet fallacious view is that an each-way bet is only worthwhile about a horse with a starting price of at least 5–1.

This point can also be demonstrated by using probability ratios. Firstly, it should be appreciated that when statisticians apply these particular ratios to horse racing situations they assume, despite the fact that logically one can only do this when assessing a handicap, that all the horses taking part in races have equal chances of success. Indeed, in statistical text books, for the sake of illustrative convenience, such experts frequently apply their favoured theories of probability to an eight horse race in which they suggest that the runners involved could finish in 336 different ways that would affect win and each-way wagers. Of these 336 'outcomes', it is usually claimed that 42 would involve a win for any runner, that 84 would present it with an opportunity to be placed and that 210 would feature its failure to reach the frame. What is significant here is that if a horse were to experience such a statistical 'fate' in 336 races and it went to post at much shorter odds than 5–1 – say at 5–2, for example – *less* would be lost by supporting it throughout each-way, than backing it to win with equivalent sums. This particular conclusion again runs quite contrary to popular belief. So, interestingly, does not only the general principle that each-way wagering represents a sizeable saving over equivalent win only betting when a *short* rather than a long starting price is involved, but also its corollary – that betting to win on horses returned at more than 5–1 is more *advantageous* in the long run than supporting them each-way.

Confused? – well, all should become clear from columns five and six in the table on page 180.

'Probably performances of handicapper contesting 336 eight runner handicaps	Starting price returned on each occasion	Result of wagering £2 win at such odds throughout (pre-tax)	Result of wagering £1 e.w. at such odds thoughout (pre-tax)	Proportion expressed as percentage by which each way improves on result of equivalent win only wagering	as percentage by which win only betting improves on result of equivalent each way wagering
42 wins	10-1	+ £840	+£504	–	–
84 placed	10-1	–£588	+ £84	–	–
210 unplaced	10-1		–£420	–	–
Overall outcome	–	+£252	+£168	–	50%
42 wins	5-1	+£420	+£252	–	–
84 placed	5-1	–£588	level	–	–
210 unplaced	5-1		–£420	–	–
Overall outcome	–	–£168	–£168	–	–
42 wins	5-2	+£210	+£126	–	–
84 placed	5-2	–£588	– £42	–	–
210 unplaced	5-2		–£420	–	–
Overall outcome	–	–£378	–£336	12%	–
42 wins	Evens	+ £84	+£50.40	–	–
84 placed	Evens	–£588	–£67.20	–	–
210 unplaced	Evens	–£588	–£420	–	–
Overall outcome	–	–£504	–£436.80	14%	–

The assumptions featured in the calculations on page 184 presuppose that any runner in an eight horse handicap has a rather *slight* 12½% prospect of success, or a 126 in 336 chance of being placed because any of its rivals is just as likely to triumph. In practice, of course, because some contestants happen to be favoured by certain conditions that the handicapper has been unable to anticipate, such as the going and the draw, such a 'pessimistic' statistical assumption is probably inappropriate. Certainly such an unpromising prediction cannot be made about other types of races, since their rather arbitrary entry conditions bestow distinctly unequal opportunities on their contestants which may, in fact, greatly favour some of them. Such events, of course, are non-handicaps which by definition feature nothing (apart from the application of broad generalisations about the respective abilities of horses of certain ages or sexes) that is expressly designed to equalise the chances of their contestants.

Should this be doubted, the following example of entry conditions for a non-handicap should be studied:

Gold Seal Oaks (Group I) **1½m**

£100000 added to stakes **for three yr old fillies only** £375 to enter £375 ex if entry confirmed: Wts: 9st each EVER READY LIMITED have generously sponsored this race, the prize money for which includes a trophy value £3500 for the winning owner THERE WILL BE A PARADE FOR THIS RACE Closed on Feb 28 total ent 133 Forfeit declared for 110 The remainder pay forfeit. ft dec for 121

Penalty value £101,475; 2nd £37,973.75, 3rd £18,236.88, 4th £7,939.37

Many deductions have now been made from the above table. What these seem to suggest is that if each-way betting is more advantageous than win only wagering on handicappers starting at fairly short odds, it will be far more so if it concerns similarly priced horses running in non-handicaps. If, moreover, on the basis of exhaustive form and time calculations, such contestants appear to be greatly favoured by the unequal opportunities presented by the non-handicap situation, their each-way claims should be seriously considered.

However, I must stress that not all the horses you carefully select and then find are given market quotations of less than 5–1 against their chances of winning prestigious non-handicaps like the Oaks or St. Leger, for example, should be supported each-way. In practice, this is only really worthwhile if a *certain number of runners* goes to post. Indeed, if there are more than nine contestants or seven, rather than six, this type of betting will tend to favour the bookmaker rather than the backer.

It is prudent to wager each-way for one further reason – the generous treatment you receive if your selection – say a 2–1 chance in a non-handicap of eight runners – only manages to be placed. What you will then find is that a bookmaker will take the price that he has quoted against the horse *winning* the race and conveniently, but arbitrarily, divide it by a fifth. By working to such a fixed fraction he makes life easier for his settler but, in so doing, he may substantially underestimate the actual chances a horse has of being placed, so as to give something away to the backer. After all, an each-way bet on a 2–1 chance that finished second or third will bring in a return (less a small contribution to the Chancellor) that will enable you to recoup 40% of what you have lost. This is no mean saving and compares very favourably with the paltry dividends the Tote can pay to those of its patrons who bet win and place on short-priced horses that head the market in non-handicaps and are opposed by an appropriate number of rivals.

There are, of course, sound reasons for this. Firstly, the total pool from which winning place dividends are paid will have been depleted by deductions that have to be made to cover operating expenses and tax liabilities. Secondly, this pool is only made up of a sum accruing from what is a limited number of losing place wagers. Finally, of course, the number of Tote patrons who have been astute enough to appreciate the excellent place prospects of such short-priced non-handicappers is likely to be large and thus, each one of them has to accept a rather small share of an inconsiderable sum. In contrast, those who bet each-way with bookmakers are paid a price that has not been trimmed on account of the identical behaviour of other punters, but has actually been apportioned by others who have placed quite different and, in actual fact, losing bets.

Thus, the serious investor should only resort to each-way betting when the number of runners in the non-handicap he is considering and the price quoted against his selection both lie within the parameters that have been outlined above. If only one of these criteria is met, *win only wagers* should be made, just as they should when ten, five or even fewer runners face the starter. As for races with seven runners, win only wagering is similarly recommended, with the proviso that it is worth considering a place only interest on the Tote about an animal whose market price and chances of reaching the frame are both considerable.

When betting *to win,* apart from the size of your stake, the only other decision that has to be made is whether to do business with a bookmaker or to patronise the Tote. Since the latter first began trading on the July course at Newmarket in 1929, its adherents have claimed that it serves the winning punter rather better than the bookmakers, while its detractors have declared that this is decidedly not the case. Rather than delve into this contentious topic, what will be considered here is the pertinent fact that the British backer, like his fortunate counterpart in South Africa, Australia, Belgium and India, can choose between becoming involved with two very different operations which, because they have to compete for his trade, offer him what amounts to a bewildering array of quite distinctive, and even decidedly exotic, betting possibilities. Many of the latter, whether they are the creations of bookmakers or Tote officials, involve the laying of large prices about highly unlikely multiple occurrences – that most lucrative of ways in which the greed of punters has traditionally been exploited on the turf. Some of these wagers that prove so tempting to the unwary tyro can take very complex and subtle forms.

Currently, for example, bookmakers offer the backers the 'Heinz' which appropriately presents him with 57 ways of winning, if the six horses he nominates win their races and so produce 15 doubles, 20 trebles, 15 four horse accumulators, 6 five horse accumulators, as well as one six horse accumulator! For other backers who believe, contrary to the actual experience of most jockeys, that 'going through the card' is quite possible, the Tote jackpot is available. This will also bring quite astronomic returns to those who can name the winners of the first six races at specified meetings. Such royal roads to ruin, rather than fortune, lie 'beyond the pale' for the true professional. As one who automatically shops around bookmakers' boards for the best price available, he is merely appreciative of the possibility, denied his counterparts in most countries, of being able to take his trade to the Tote when it suits him.

Deciding when to adopt this particular tactic is fairly difficult. However, research into racing returns suggests that, generally speaking, patronising the Tote in *particular circumstances* can be a better proposition than placing equivalent bets with bookmakers. Suggestions have been made that on certain courses, Tote dividends generally pay rather better than the starting prices that are returned, while extensive research suggests that at major meetings, especially top-class fixtures that extend over several days (like the Royal meeting at Ascot, York's August Festival, 'Glorious' Goodwood and Chester's May meeting) it generally pays to place win only bets with bookmakers. This is because the on-course betting market is at its strongest at such meetings at which some of the largest individual bets of the season will be placed with bookmakers, who, in the main rings at least, will tempt large crowds made up of many regular racegoers with highly competitive prices.

Moreover, if a minor meeting, particularly one that is held at the beginning of the week or on the same day as a much more prestigious fixture, is rather poorly attended then the Tote pool will be diminutive and thus susceptible to distortion should connections place a sizeable commission at Tote odds. The 'ripples' in the pool that are caused by such a wager can substantially reduce a winning dividend.

In contrast, in the summer, if a large crowd of 'occasional' racegoers is found in the cheaper enclosures at holiday meetings or evening fixtures held on lowly racecourses, the Tote is likely to do good business and thus its dividends may well dwarf the starting prices that are returned. Again, if you remember that you always receive a high Tote dividend if your perceptive judgement has not been shown by the majority of those patronising the 'machine', this will explain why, in general, if you want to back a horse to win that this particular group of betters will probably pass over, because bookmakers have given it a pessimistic quotation in excess of 5–1, you should make your wager on the Tote. Again, if you find that your wish to bet each-way is frustrated by the very short price that is apportioned to your selection, then it will be wise to strike a straight win bet away from the Tote window.

Before some rather sophisticated betting strategies involving win only wagering are examined, it may prove useful if some other circumstances in which Tote investment usually proves profitable are considered. In the main, if you can detect a particular reason, or more than one, why the claims of the horse or its connections are likely to be ignored, you have also probably identified a reason for patronising the Tote. For example, runners from stables which do not enjoy a strong local following on a racecourse, seldom send winners to it, or are otherwise out of favour because they are small, foreign, unfashionable or infrequently successful, should be supported on the Tote if their market quotations reflect these unpromising portents.

There are further instances when you should consider taking on 'the machine' rather than one's bookmaker. On occasion, you may find that the dealings of the latter feature a so-called 'corner horse' – one unquoted in newspapers' starting price forecasts which, unexpectedly, figures as a market leader in the opening betting 'show'. It should be backed on the Tote, as should a 'springer' – a horse whose initially rather long odds are trimmed by a substantial proportion.

The following is a guide to courses on which it is possible to say that, generally speaking, it should pay the backer either to bet (a) with bookmakers or (b) with 'the machine':

Flat Courses

(a) Ascot, Ayr, Bath, Brighton, Carlisle, Catterick, Chepstow, Chester, Edinburgh, Epsom, Goodwood, Kempton, Newcastle, Newmarket, Sandown, Warwick, Wolverhampton, Yarmouth, York.

(b) Beverley, Doncaster, Hamilton, Haydock, Folkestone, Leicester, Lingfield, Newbury, Nottingham, Pontefract, Redcar, Ripon, Salisbury, Thirsk, Windsor.

National Hunt Courses

(a) Bangor, Cheltenham, Devon, Hexham, Kelso, Newton Abbot, Plumpton, Sedgefield, Stratford, Wetherby, Wincanton, Worcester.

(b) Cartmel, Fakenham, Fontwell, Hereford, Huntingdon, Ludlow, Market Rasen, Perth, Southwell.

In contrast, circumstances may arise which are conducive to advanced strategies of win only wagering. For example, it may on occasion transpire that when the winning chances, not only of your leading fancy on form and time but also of its main rivals, are translated into odds, these all prove shorter than the actual rates on offer in the market. Much more frequently, the backer may feel really confident that a race is going to be won by one of two or three runners and may wish to avoid reproaching himself if he makes the wrong choice between them. In such situations, it may be appropriate to attempt the ambitious strategy of betting 'coupled'. This is a ploy often adopted by professionals on-course, although seldom do they go to quite the same lengths as the legendary Charles Hannan. He was a leviathan gambler of the 1920's who would spread as much as £10,000 between three horses in one race in the firm belief that one would oblige and bring in a handsome profit.

It is, fortunately, quite simple to determine the odds that result from this subtle tactic and to calculate the stakes that are necessary to effect it.

Firstly you:

(i) Multiply the two prices together and then subtract *one* from what results. This gives the left-hand side of the odds.

(ii) Then you add one point to each price and then total the two; (i) against (ii) gives the rate of 'coupled' odds against the two contestants.

In practice, this procedure is far simpler than it sounds, as the following example should confirm:

Horse A Board Price 2–1
Horse B Board Price 6–1
Part (i) of calculation as above
2 x 6 = 12
12 – 1 = 11
Part (ii) of calculation
(2 + 1) = 3
+ (6 + 1) = 7
= 10

(i) against (ii) = 11–10, which are the 'coupled' odds against Horse A or B winning the race.

If such a calculation produces a rate of odds in excess of even money, this represents good value. Indeed, the backer must ensure that the coupled odds he is taking are long enough to justify the outlay this ploy of taking a saver actually entails. If a long odds-on quotation results from the above calculation, you should not risk losing the large sums you have to stake in order to make this 'coupled' bet.

Some punters who favour this sophisticated wagering technique may seek a certain return if one or other of the horses involved is successful. In this case, what they need is a quick and convenient way of determining how much to stake. Fortunately, this can be found in the table of odds expressed as percentages:

Odds Available	Percentage Equivalent
100–1	0.99
66–1	1.49
50–1	1.96
40–1	2.44
33–1	2.94
25–1	3.85
22–1	4.35
20–1	4.76
19–1	5.00
18–1	5.26
17–1	5.56
16–1	5.88
15–1	6.25
14–1	6.67
13–1	7.14
12–1	7.67
11–1	8.33
10–1	9.09
9–1	10.00
8–1	11.11
15–2	11.76
7–1	12.50
13–2	13.50
6–1	14.29
11–2	15.38
5–1	16.67
9–2	18.18
4–1	20.00
7–2	22.22
100–30	23.08
3–1	25.00
11–4	26.67
5–2	28.57
95–40	29.63
9–4	30.77
2–1	33.33
15–8	34.78

Odds Available	Percentage Equivalent
7–4	36.36
13–8	38.10
6–4	40.00
11–8	42.11
5–4	44.44
6–5	45.45
11–10	47.62
Evens	50.00
10–11	52.38
5–6	54.55
4–5	55.56
8–11	57.89
4–6	60.00
8–13	61.90
4–7	63.64
8–15	65.71
1–2	66.67
4–9	69.23
40–95	70.37
2–5	71.43
4–11	73.33
1–3	75.00
30–100	76.92
2–7	77.78
1–4	80.00
2–9	81.82
1–5	83.33
2–11	84.62
1–6	85.71
2–13	86.67
1–7	87.50
2–15	88.24
1–8	88.89

All you need to do is to take the percentage figures that appear in this table as the various sums involved if your coupled bet is to bring a return of 100 points including the stake.

Alternatively, the following 'field money' table can be used:

FIELD MONEY TABLE (to the nearest stake unit)

Odds	Stake	Odds	Stake	Odds	Stake	Odds	Stake
50–1	2	7–2	22	Evens	50	2–7*	78
33–1	3	10–3	23	20–21	51	1–4	80
25–1	4	3–1	25	10–11	52	2–9	81
20–1	5	11–4	27	5–6	54	1–5	83
16–1	6	5–2	29	4–5	56	2–11	85
14–1	7	95–40	30	8–11	58	1–6	86
12–1	8	9–4	31	4–6	60	1–7	87
10–1	9	2–1	33	8–13	62	1–8	89
9–1	10	15–8	35	4–7	64	1–10	91
8–1	11	7–4	36	8–15	65	1–12	92
15–2	12	13–8	38	1–2	67	1–14	93
7–1	13	6–4	40	4–9	69	1–16	94
6–1	14	11–8	42	40–95	70	1–20	95
11–2	15	5–4	44	2–5	71	1–25	96
5–1	17	6–5	46	4–11	73	1–33	97
9–2	19	11–10	48	1–3	75	1–50	98
4–1	20	21–20	49	3–10	77		

(* In practice, bookmakers seldom quote odds which are shorter than this particular rate. Such quotations are included for the sake of interest.)

The field money table is, in fact, a simplification of the extremely precise figures shown on the previous page. This is necessary since, if these were allowed to determine the various stakes that comprise a coupled bet, a racecourse bookmaker could be forgiven for calling the parentage of the backer into question. Imagine approaching such a hard-bitten businessman and requesting a £33.33p win bet on Horse 'A' at 2–1, and then trying to place an even more precise £14.29p on Horse 'B' at 6–1.

Fortunately, the stickler for figures can take such bizarre business to a licensed betting office which may be actually located on the track itself. This particular strategy will at least give you the chance, without arousing any controversy, to stake very precise sums at 'board' prices which, significantly, are the only odds available off-course that allow such a would-be professional to predict the precise outcome of a prospective wager.

By this point it may have become clear that betting 'coupled' is a ploy that is fraught with practical difficulty. A further problem may arise if you do not have the table of odds as percentages or the field money table in your possession. If this is the case, a simple formula can be used to calculate what needs to be staked to strike a 'coupled' bet. All you need to do is to divide the sum of the two figures that feature in a rate of odds into 100 and multiply the result by the 'stake' side of the odds.

The following example, featuring a coupled bet on three horses, should make this clear:

Horse 'X' at 7–4
7 + 4 = 11
11 divided into 100 = 9 (approx.)
9 x 4 = 36 points to be staked.
Horse 'Y' at 3–1
3 + 1 = 4
4 divided into 100 = 25
25 x 1 = 25 points to be staked.
Horse 'Z' at 5–1

5 + 1 = 6
6 divided into 100 = 17 (approx.)
17 x 1 = 17 points to be staked.

Thus, a total of 78 points would need to be invested (36 points at 7–4, 25 points at 3–1 and 17 points at 5–1), in the hope that one of the three horses involved will 'oblige' and bring a return of 100 points. The profits margin here would thus be 22 points or 29% – well in excess of percentages which, when they are trading equitably, bookmakers are quite content to accept as their 'mark up' or profit margin.

STRATEGY 37:

Staking for Success

Having suggested certain approaches to the problem of selection and wagering, it is now time to consider how to increase potential profits through *sensible staking*. Firstly, it should be realised that, like any successful bookmaker or other intelligent businessman, the serious backer should have substantial capital behind him and never risk too great a proportion of it on any one speculative undertaking. Initially, you should accumulate a bank whose size should be determined by what you can bear to lose over the season-long trading period. This particular sum should be regarded as made up of 100 stake units. This, incidentally, has the added advantage of facilitating calculations involving profits to turnover, which, of course, constantly preoccupy any businesslike bookmaker.

Say, for example, the aspiring professional has accumulated a bank of £1,000, the unlikely, yet of course conceivable, loss of which he would be prepared to accept. This sum should then be equally divided into a 'capital' fund and a 'betting' fund. The next stage is to consider what possible functions the betting fund may have to carry out and for how long. This will call for a degree of foresight on the backer's part that can only be forthcoming if you direct your hindsight to past seasons and the patterns of results these have featured. The problem here, of course, is that you may not have kept complete and detailed records of your systematic wagering over a number of seasons that is sufficiently long for conclusions of any validity and practical value to be drawn. Thus, I would suggest that you consult the only continuously published records of the performances of horse racing selections – the 'naps' of newspaper correspondents whose success or lack of it is tabulated so meticulously six times a week in the *Sporting Life* or *Racing Post* simply because they qualify as entries in one or both of the tipping contests that these racing dailies organise during the season and decide on its last day in November.

The precise tabular form that these particular records take can be seen from the example below:

RACING POST

tote National Press Challenge

Sponsored by the Tote and Charles Heidsieck Champagne

EACH competitor starts the month with a theoretical bank of £100, from which £1 is staked AT TOTE ODDS on his selection in every race at meetings for which Racing Post carries a full selection box (usually all meetings except on Bank Holidays). The tipster with the largest bank at the end of the month wins £100 of Tote betting vouchers plus a magnum of Charles Heidsieck champagne. Racing Post will donate the winning total to a racing charity of the winner's choice. At the end of the year the tipster with the largest cumulative bank, based on Tote odds, will receive his winning total (plus the £100 added each month) and a trophy, both donated by The Tote, plus a jeroboam of Charles Heidsieck champagne. SP columns are shown for comparative purposes only. ● Compiled by DATASPORT

ALL RACES – RECORD FOR THE MONTH					YEAR TO DATE (from March 1)					NAPS (for information only)				
£100 BANK TOTE ODDS (and SP)		NEWSPAPER and TIPSTER	WINS-TIPS		CUMULATIVE BANK TOTE ODDS (and SP)		WINS-TIPS		FAVOURITES TIPPED	TODAY'S NAP		TOTAL WINS-NAPS	£1 BET AT SP	CURRENT SEQUENCE
£171.00	(£164.69)	**TODAY** *Henry Rix*	82-222	27%	£950	(£540)	1025-3719	27%	40%	**Sanawi**	2.00 Gwood	31-167	£-6.34	2L
£133.00	(£166.15)	**GUARDIAN** *Chris Hawkins*	66-221	30%	£132	(£270)	1090-3729	29%	52%	**Reference Light**	2.30 Donc	45-166	−£31.90	4L
£127.30	(£131.85)	**D EXPRESS** *Bendex*	53-220	24%	£423	(£459)	1093-3724	29%	46%	**Reference Light**	2.30 Donc	61-163	£24.45	3L
£118.90	(£119.36)	**D MAIL** *Robin Goodfellow*	61-217	28%	£283	(£363)	1103-3743	29%	50%	**Snurge**	3.40 Donc	37-167	−£24.79	5L
£114.90	(£127.70)	**RACING POST** *Spotlight*	65-221	29%	£285	(£358)	1118-3740	29%	53%	**Nayland**	4.15 Donc	48-168	£37.54	2W
£104.90	(£107.09)	**INDEPENDENT** *Hyperion*	54-220	24%	£290	(£347)	1000-3725	27%	44%	**Sanawi**	2.00 Gwood	25-166	−£36.00	4L
£93.00	(£93.81)	**THE SUN** *Templegate*	54-219	24%	£137	(£251)	1082-3719	29%	53%	**Hellenic**	3.40 Donc	30-166	−£20.50	1L
£87.00	(£102.49)	**D STAR** *Tony Lewis*	62-223	27%	£206	(£386)	1090-3734	29%	49%	**Nayland**	4.15 Donc	39-163	−£14.35	1W
£74.40	(£87.95)	**TELEGRAPH** *Tony Stafford*	63-220	28%	£431	(£417)	1087-3727	29%	49%	**Where's Carol**	5.15 Donc	34-165	−£48.44	1L
£58.10	(£63.74)	**SP LIFE** *Man on Spot*	52-220	23%	£ 95	(£171)	1083-3730	29%	54%	**Platonique**	5.45 Donc	30-164	−£24.10	4L
£51.80	(£59.26)	**RACING POST** *Diomed*	55-217	25%	£327	(£370)	1167-3711	31%	50%	**Hellenic**	3.40 Donc	50-164	−£13.25	2L
£31.10	(£40.85)	**TIMES** *Mandarin*	61-260	22%	£116	(£239)	1150-3785	30%	56%	**Unanimous**	5.15 Donc	54-165	−£30.00	4L
£30.00	(£53.25)	**RACING POST** *Postmark*	49-217	22%	£107	(£287)	999-3588	27%	43%	**Hellenic**	3.40 Donc	52-165	£-6.10	2W
£29.20	(£38.71)	**D MIRROR** *Newsboy*	50-221	22%	£110	(£184)	1082-3715	28%	52%	**Affordable**	5.15 Donc	35-168	−£14.90	3L

★Hyperion and Templegate were both on the mark yesterday with Wallinglen Lane (Tote £19.70).

Today's Most Popular Selection: MULCIBER 3.20 Chepstow and BEAU ROSE 4.15 Worcester 13 tips

Source: The Racing Post

At this point, in defence of those correspondents who may at particular stages of the season find themselves at the bottom of such a table, it should be stressed that newspaper tipsters make a 'nap' selection every day and that many of them are obliged to do so in the race that their editors feel will interest the majority of their readers. Since such an event is frequently something of a lottery, in that it is commonly the most competitive and valuable handicap of the day, it is hardly surprising that research into newspaper 'naps' tables over several seasons shows that, in general, only one in four tipsters (and usually different ones each year) manage to achieve profit figures by the end of the season. Such research also indicates that over a complete season, losing runs commonly exceed 20 and may even extend as far as 30. Indeed, not even the spectacular 40–1 success of Tearaway, his appropriately named nap for the Manchester November Handicap, held on the last day of the 1955 season, was able to disguise the fact that Claude Harrison, 'Carlton' of the *Daily Despatch*, the eventual winner of the Sporting Life Challenge Cup, had previously tipped no less than 28 consecutive losers! This can be seen in the following *Sporting Life* table which covers the complete 1955 season:

From March 21 to November 12

				Lngst.	Seq.	Cons.	£1 Level Stakes		
	W.	L.	N.R.	Wins	Lsrs.	Lsrs.	£	s.	d.
Daily Dispatch (Carlton) ..	41	110	22	3	28	0	+46	14	1
Irish Times (Brown Jack) ..	39	126	26	5	12	4	+26	13	8
Daily Mail (Robin Goodfellow)..	56	101	17	4	9	4	+ 6	19	10
Greyhound Express (Winco) ..	75	94	5	5	7	1	+ 6	2	8
Birmingham Gazette (Stable Boy)	54	120	17	4	11	1	+ 2	2	7
Sporting Life (Warren Hill) ..	49	108	12	4	13	0	− 1	9	2
Sporting Life (Augur)	57	106	11	8	13	1	− 3	2	11
Liverpool Post (Argus)	49	129	13	4	11	6	− 3	7	10
News Chronicle (Capt. Heath) ..	50	117	7	4	16	1	− 6	4	2
Daily Mirror (Newsboy).. ..	37	125	12	4	13	1	− 7	8	10
Sporting Life (Solon)	56	103	15	4	9	1	−10	1	3
Irish Independent (Capt. Keen)..	47	125	19	4	12	5	−16	9	10
Daily Express (The Scout) ..	52	114	7	4	15	4	−23	12	2
Daily Record (Garry Owen) ..	43	114	17	3	9	5	−24	10	8
Sporting Life (Man on the Spot)..	49	113	12	4	14	1	−25	19	2
Morning Advertiser (Arion) ..	51	113	9	3	10	5	−28	5	11
Daily Herald (Templegate) ..	48	115	11	5	18	18	−29	3	2
Birmingham Post (Veritas) ..	39	139	13	3	12	10	−29	11	11
Daily Sketch (Gimcrack) ..	43	121	10	4	15	6	−32	7	10
Daily Telegraph (Hotspur) ..	50	113	11	5	9	1	−32	11	3
Yorkshire Post (The Duke) ..	46	131	14	3	11	3	−37	1	2
Sporting Chronicle (Kettledrum)	57	110	7	5	9	1	−49	10	10

Source: Sporting Life

Hypothetically, if Claude Harrison had begun supporting his own selections at the commencement of his protracted losing run and had doubled his stakes after each successive loser, he would, after his fifteenth losing wager, have lost 32,767 points. Furthermore, had the bank at his disposal been sufficiently gargantuan both to fund a further 13 unsuccessful bets, bear the eventual loss of 268, 435, 455 points suffered before the arrival of Tearaway and to provide an equivalent sum to support this particular runner, he would still have had to find a bookmaker to do business with him. At odds of 40–1 this would have actually involved an eventual payout of 121, 005, 853, 696 points.

What emerges from the astronomically high hypothetical sums that are cited above is that when a long losing run is encountered at some stage or other, as it inevitably will be in the fullness of time, you should be already implementing a staking plan which will drastically reduce, rather than frighteningly increase, the rate at which recurring losses erode your original profits. Such a plan will only be sound if it is capable of withstanding what is the most debilitating experience it is possible for the backer to undergo – *being beset by a prolonged run of losers from the very outset of his betting operations.* 'Carlton' after all would not have won the *Sporting Life* Trophy and his prize of £100 had his now notorious losing run occurred in the spring. That this particular unprecedented sequence was the sequel to a profitable period that had extended as far as the early autumn of 1955, was the crucial underlying reason why Tearaway was ultimately able to carry Claude Harrison well clear of his nearest rivals.

The staking plan that will be shortly described will enable you to endure a long losing run, irrespective of whether this occurs initially or eventually. This is because it features a 'betting' bank of

500 points made up of fifty 10 point stake units which, if wagered in a carefully prescribed way, would actually allow a losing run like Carlton's to be borne even if, disastrously, it were to occur at the start of the season. This plan, in fact, would permit as many as 35 consecutive losers to be supported from the commencement of betting operations before any inroads would have to be made into your remaining 'capital' fund of a further 500 points.

The betting fund, if it can stand such an initial onslaught, will, of course, prove more than sufficient to withstand the far more probable and less spectacular long losing sequences that, despite the basic soundness of your selection procedures, as a realistic professional you know will inexplicably arise and have to be weathered. This plan will also facilitate your rapid recovery from a losing run by ensuring that sizeable stakes are placed on horses that win once it has ended. It also prevents any excessive 'playing up' of winnings in the naive belief that these somehow provide a propitious pointer to future prospects.

Indeed, your careful study of form, scrutiny of race times, analysis of the betting market and research into trainers' behaviour may incline you to take a fairly rosy view of probability, but you should avoid any staking procedure which is based upon it. This is why the instructions that now follow fail to feature very much in the way of staking arrangements that involve increasing stakes after winners, since the success of these always depends on the dubious assumption that any winning run is likely to prove extensive. A mere glance at the figures containing naps tables in the *Sporting Life* that detail the longest losing runs of newspaper correspondents at particular points in racing seasons, should suffice to disabuse any serious backer of the belief that nothing invariably succeeds like success in the business of making horse racing selections.

The staking plan is operated as follows:

You begin with a stake of two units (£20 in the case of a 50 point betting bank of £500). If your first selection wins, two points are also staked on its successor. (Incidentally, odds-on winners should be treated as non-runners.) If the first bet loses, your second stake becomes three points. Should five consecutive losers be experienced at this or any other stage, your outlay should be reduced to a single point which should be staked until a winner is found at evens or better. Rather than jeopardise the resultant profit by subsequent reckless wagering, you subtract two points from the stake placed on this winner, if it was from four to six points, three points if it was from seven to eleven points, or four points if it was from 12 or more stake units. Apart from the precautionary single point that is always staked after five consecutive losers (the safeguard that would have protected Carlton's supporters in 1955), the minimum stake is always two points.

When the long losing run has ended and that elusive winner has at last been found, it is time to increase your stake. Accordingly, you should look back to where you began staking a single point and add a single point to that last losing 'increased' stake. This sounds rather complicated, so for the sake of clarification, an example of the plan in operation is given on page 205. Conveniently it shows both how a stake is reduced after five consecutive losers and how an odds-on winner is treated as a non-runner.

The data it features relates to the mid-season performance of a newspaper tipster whose previous selections, with the considerable assistance of the staking plan, had produced a healthy profit.

Horse Win or Lose	Points Staked (Bank £500)	Amount Invested	Win	Lose	Running Before Win	Total Tax Lose
		£.	£. p.	£. p.	£. p.	£. p.
Brought forward						3382.50
L	6	60		60.00	3322.50	
L	7	70		70.00	3252.50	
W 11-10	8	80	88.00		3340.50	
L	5	50		50.00	3290.50	

Horse Win or Lose	Points Staked (Bank £500)	Amount Invested	Win	Lose	Running Before Win	Total Tax Lose
		£	£. p.	£. p.	£. p.	£. p.
L	6	60		60.00	3230.50	
L	7	70		70.00	3160.50	
L	8	80		80.00	3080.50	
W 2-5 +	9	90	36.00		3116.50	
L	1	10		90.00	3026.50	
L	1	10		10.00	3006.50	
W 2-1	1	10	20.00		3026.50	
W 7-2	10	100	350.00		3376.50	
L	7	70		70.00	3306.50	
L	8	80		80.00	3226.50	
W3-1	9	90	270.00		3496.50	
L	6	60		60.00	3436.50	
W 11-8	7	70	96.25		3532.75	
L	4	40		40.00	3492.75	
W 5-1	5	50	250.00		3742.75	
L	2	20		20.00		20.00
L	3	30		30.00		50.00
L	4	40		40.00		90.00
L	5	50		50.00		140.00
L	6	60		60.00		200.00

Should the sceptical reader point out that the above results look impressive merely because they are the sequel to a series of particularly profitable wagers, they will be 're-cast' as a continuation of an initial losing run that leads to a single point, as opposed to eight stake units, being placed on the first 11–10 winner that they feature. This should demonstrate how the plan can help the patient backer who has to make minor inroads into his capital reserve before progress is made towards eventual profitability.

Horse Win or Lose	Points Staked (Bank £500)	Amount Invested	Win	Lose	Running Before Win	Total Tax Lose
		£	£. p.	£. p.	£. p.	£. p.
L	1	10		10.00		210.00
W 11-10	1	10	11.00			199.00
L	7	70		70.00		269.00
L	8	80		80.00		349.00
L	9	90		90.00		439.00
L	10	100		100.00		539.00
W 2-5	10	100		40.00		499.00
L	10	100		100.00		599.00
L	1	10		10.00		609.00
L	1	10		10.00		619.00
W 2-1	1	10	20.00			599.00
W 7-2	11	110	385.00			214.00
L	8	80		80.00		294.00
L	9	90		90.00		384.00
W 3-1	10	100	300.00			84.00
L	7	70		70.00		154.00
W 11-8	8	80	110.00			44.00
L	5	50		50.00		94.00
W 5-1	6	60	300.00		205.00	

Finally, it should be stressed that any professional must be prepared for 'lean' periods involving long losing runs, not because these are expected but because this is prudent. Indeed, if you make selections on the lines suggested, rather than on the difficult and restrictive ones that constrain newspaper correspondents, you should, barring particular bad luck, make a level stake profit which the above staking plan will handsomely augment.

It should be noted that any profits that accrue from the implementation of this plan should be divided equally between the 'betting' and 'capital' funds. Then, if and when the latter is found to have increased by 200%, it will be time to double the size of the units you have hitherto staked so methodically. In other words, like any shrewd businessman, you should plough back a significant proportion of any profits and put them to work in potentially even more rewarding ways; such re-investment of profits is, after all, a standard ploy of the successful entrepreneur.

More Titles From Rushmere Wynne

Rushmere Wynne specialises in the publication of popular and investment books. Our current list includes the following titles:

THE INVESTORS' HANDBOOK
by Maggie Drummond
(£6.95 Paperback) ISBN 0 948035 04 8
An excellent introduction to the basics of stockmarket trading.

THE PRIVATE INVESTOR'S GUIDE TO THE STOCKMARKET
by Neil Stapley
(£8.95 Paperback) ISBN 0 948035 11 0
One of the best introductions to the stockmarket yet written by a leading private client stockbroker. The book explains how to build your share portfolio, how to evaluate shares, how to assess risk and much much more.

PROFIT FROM YOUR PC

How to use a personal computer to buy and sell shares

by David Linton

(£9.99 Paperback) ISBN 0 948035 16 1

A leading PC software expert explains how you can set up your own data capture system allowing you to develop an integrated investment strategy which combines fundamental analysis and charting. The book includes a FREE stockmarket PC game: PROFIT FOR WINDOWS.

THE INDEX OPTION

by Neil Osborne

The Private Investor's Route to Stockmarket Wealth

(£14.99 Hardback) ISBN 0 948035 24 2

A London market trader explains the profitable use of the Index Option for the modern private investor. Book includes free demo disk for Traded Options evaluation program.

30 WAYS TO MAKE MONEY IN FRANCHISING

by Roger Beard

(£7.99 Paperback) ISBN 0 948035 29 3

What does franchising involve? How do you get started? Roger Beard gives you all the vital information you need on every aspect of franchising. A comprehensive guide for all those thinking of taking the plunge.

THE COMPLETE GUIDE TO PERSONAL PENSIONS

by Jenny Harris

(£7.99 Paperback) ISBN 0 948035 30 7

Written in a jargon-free style, this invaluable book explains just what you can expect from the State, how to assess a company pension scheme, executive pensions and how to take advantage of personal pensions.

HOW TO MAKE A KILLING IN PENNY SHARES
by Michael Walters
(£9.99 Paperback) ISBN 0 948035 20 X
Already sold 50,000, this is the up-dated version of the best seller written by the deputy City editor of the *Daily Mail,* Michael Walters.

PROFIT OF THE PLUNGE
by Simon Cawkwell
(£9.99 Paperback) ISBN 0 948035 17 X
This book was banned by the judge in the Maxwell trial. Now available, it tells the secrets of one of the most active short-sellers of all time including his dealings with the Maxwell Communication Corporation. If you are interested in the stockmarket, this book is a 'must'.

CHARTERS ON CHARTING:
How to improve your stockmarket decision making
by David Charters
(£12.95 Hardback) ISBN 0 948035 21 8
Already on its third reprint, this book has become a classic. It explains how charting works. Described by *the Investors' book club* as "the best charting book for the private investor we have seen."

HOW TO MAKE A KILLING IN THE ALTERNATIVE INVESTMENT MARKET

by Michael Walters

(£9.95 Paperback) ISBN 0 948035 14 5

The deputy City editor of the *Daily Mail*, Michael Walters, writes the third in his best selling trilogy of books for his numerous readers.

TRADED OPTIONS – A PRIVATE INVESTOR'S GUIDE: How to invest more profitably

by Peter Temple

(£16.95 Hardback) ISBN 0 948035 06 4

Written by the author and journalist, Peter Temple, the book explains traded options in a step-by-step style. It is sponsored by LIFFE and ProShare.

EVERY WOMAN'S GUIDE TO PERSONAL FINANCE

by Rosanna Spero

(£9.99 Paperback) ISBN 0 948035 15 3

Daily Mail journalist Rosanna Spero provides a practical guide for women of all ages and stages in the management of their finances.

INVESTMENT CLUBS: The low-risk way to stockmarket profits

by Tony Drury

(£6.99 Paperback) ISBN 0 948035 22 6

Would you like to become a successful stockmarket investor? You can, by reading this book. Experience the fun and fellowship of investing in a low-risk way, within the confines of an investment club.

BETTING TO WIN

by Luke Johnson, Hugh Osmond

(£7.99 Paperback) ISBN 0 948035 31 5

With advice on horse racing, card games, casino games, bingo, pools, dogs, slot machines, gambling with dice and of course, the National Lottery, this book will show how to improve your chances of winning by knowing the odds and analysing form.